Sonoran Borders

Threads of Friendship

Vickie LoPiccolo Jennett

Sonoran Borders
Threads of Friendship

By Vickie LoPiccolo Jennett

EDITOR: Jenifer Dick
DESIGNER: Sarah Mosher
PHOTOGRAPHY: Aaron T. Leimkuehler
ILLUSTRATION: Eric Sears
CHARTS: Alissa Christianson
TECHNICAL EDITOR: Mary Atherton
PHOTO EDITOR: Jo Ann Groves

PUBLISHED BY:
Kansas City Star Books
1729 Grand Blvd.
Kansas City, Missouri, USA 64108

First edition, first printing
ISBN: 978-1-61169-093-4

Library of Congress Control Number: 2013938143

Printed in the United States of America by Walsworth Publishing Co., Marceline, MO

To order copies, call StarInfo at (816) 234-4242.

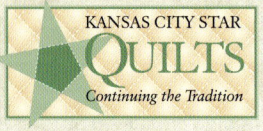

Collection of Jeremy Rowe Vintage Photography, vintagephoto.com

Table of Contents

Dedication and Acknowledgments

Dedicated in memory of two joy-filled women whose lives ended as *Sonoran Borders* was taking shape: Moira Ellen Jennett (1958–2012) and Annie Pearl Griffith (1920–2013). Your presence was a blessing to many.

ACKNOWLEDGMENTS AND GRATITUDE

First and foremost, without readers and needlework enthusiasts like you, this book would not be possible. I am profoundly grateful to all who attempt a project, savor some words or share this tale with a child who may someday ply needle and thread.

My "thank you" list is long, and no doubt I will forget someone, so chalk it up to a churning mind and know that no project could be accomplished without the unfailing love of loyal friends and folks we meet along the way.

A true debt of gratitude goes out to my husband of 36 years, who really and truly needs a big hug (or preferably a fly fishing trip away from the clutter and chaos his wife creates). He puts up with my projects and my piles, and provides encouragement when I'm saying not-so-nice things about software or stitching or whatever snag seems to arise. I am most grateful for his love and encouragement. He also taught me to appreciate the Sonoran Desert!

I include three Patricks in this list: First is Patrick Jennett, my son, who as a teen wrote me a note that read, "Write it, Mom. Just write it! A page a day." Well, many pages later, I'm still writing. Next is Patrick Whorton, my son's junior year English teacher, who taught me to appreciate irony and be honest. You are a gem of a friend and one bright man. Finally, there's

Patrick Finn, an author and instructor at Chandler-Gilbert Community College, who helped this reporter/non-fiction writer find her voice and have the courage to venture into fiction … one baby step at a time.

Then there's my partner in NeedleWorkPress, Maegan Jennett, who made me do this thing solo. Next time you're coming along for the ride. And, Linda

Danielson, whose "Little Girl" sampler helped tie together pieces of this story. Your work and love of Mexican samplers are inspiring. Thankfully, Kathy Norton and I stumbled upon one another's paths, or the finishing of projects in this book would not be nearly as delightful. Jean Lea, friend and Attic Needlework proprietor, has been my cheerleader for many years now. Your wisdom and guidance are blessings beyond compare.

Jaime Olave, a long-time compadre and a native of Sonora, Mexico, who now resides in Arizona, patiently translated phrases from English to Spanish. Regina Smith and Jean McCleery are proofreaders beyond compare. Then there's Chad Turner, who took the time to listen to my art needs and create a believable replica of 19th-century hand-drawn patterns, as well as shoot a few photographs. While we're on the subject of photography, images from Jeremy Rowe's exemplary collection definitely enhanced the tone of *Sonoran Borders.* Thanks to all of you for sharing your gifts, and for your honest and skilled assessments.

Consummate professionals best describe members of The Kansas City Star Quilts team: Editor Jenifer Dick did her best to keep me on task and teach me the nuances of compiling a "real" book. She's also a terrific taxi driver in inclement weather. Not only is designer Sarah Mosher delightfully talented, but she also "gets it." Tech editor and shop owner Mary Atherton has a keen eye. Artist Eric Sears turned amateur sketches into detailed drawings, and photographer Aaron Leimkuehler snapped some captivating close-ups. Then Jo Ann

Groves did her magic to prepare those photos for printing. Alissa Christianson's beautiful graphs will make stitching a breeze. Copy editor Diane McLendon's keen eye is a blessing. I defer to a Spanish proverb: *Even the best writer has to erase.* Thank you all!

A chance meeting with Nadiah Beekun, a philatelist with Classic Nevada Stamps and Supplies, provided essential clues about mail delivery 100+ years ago.

Carol Dickey of Kansas City's Pear Tree Design & Antiques graciously provided access to her shop at 303 E. 55th Street for on-location photos. Your kind assistance is appreciated. ✕

With profound gratitude to all who inspire and encourage creativity.

—*VLJ*

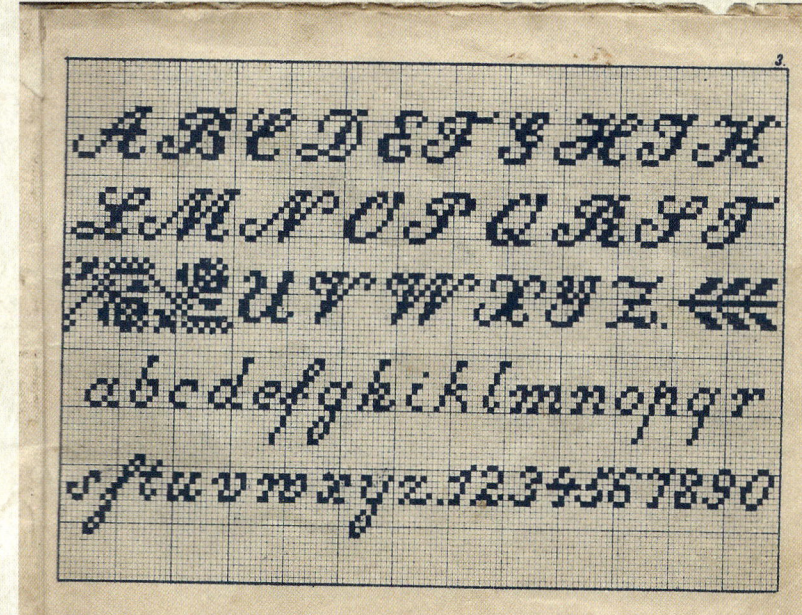

Foreword

So, you may ask, why did the granddaughter of Italian immigrants who settled in Pennsylvania decide to tell the story of families whose journeys landed them in the Western United States more than a century ago? Well, first of all, because the story is fiction, designed to accompany small needlework treasures from bygone days. While the setting could have been nearly anywhere, the choice seemed logical because of actual westward settlement that took place toward the end of the 19th century when these objects were made. Second, and perhaps far more important, since moving to Arizona as a girl, I have slowly come to experience and appreciate the rich history of our state and surrounding areas, thanks in large part to the patient and wise tutelage of a native Arizonan, my husband.

Diaries and letters attest to the fact that other than appreciating the stark, natural beauty of the desert and accomplishing hard work, music and art were among the few pleasurable pursuits that existed for women who journeyed west in the late 1800s. That is why I imagine these small handwork projects may have brought comfort and some joy to the women who managed to find the time and materials to make them. "Make-do" is a term used to describe some of the homemade sewing items (we call them "sewing smalls") that were fashioned from scraps and cast-off objects. In the process of collecting, I am often drawn to the tattered, torn and well-used artifacts, partly because they tug at my heartstrings and partly because they are what I can afford. For many years, simple handwork and related items were banished to the realm of crafts rather than art. Fortunately, in recent years, good examples have been elevated to the folk art category, and are much sought after by collectors in antiques stores and auction houses.

That said, a relatively small segment of the general population still participates in counted-thread handwork today. Every now and then I see knitters or hand-quilters — but rarely cross stitch enthusiasts — passing the time at airports or in medical waiting rooms. So, I wanted to take a stab at creating a story that may have accompanied these every-day items in the hopes that non-stitchers just might pick up these patterns and try their hand at a new pastime. Perhaps mothers, grandmothers and teachers will pass on an appreciation for this gentle art to the next generation.

Pleasant best describes my first needlework experience. We had just moved to Arizona and my mother took me to an enchanting needlepoint shop located upstairs behind a vine-covered balcony at the Royal Palms Resort and Spa. Even in its pre-renovation days, the inn exuded a delightful old-world charm. The accommodating shopkeeper patiently explained the Continental Stitch and helped me select a canvas painted with daffodils and other spring flowers. My pleasure was an opportunity to peruse the myriad wool fibers the shop offered. Wool allergies put an end to my needlepoint efforts, but an incredible palette of cottons and silks — many of them skillfully overdyed — won me over to counted cross stitch. Years of stitching on Aida cloth finally gave way to linen, and the creation of NeedleWorkPress to reproduce and adapt antique needlework charts for 21st-century stitchers.

I am most grateful for the opportunity to share these pieces of the past with you today. My hope is that handwork lives on to be shared with someone tomorrow. ✕

Introduction

That which we elect to surround ourselves with becomes the museum of our soul and the archive of our experience.

— Thomas Jefferson

Small trinkets of material culture — a friendship bracelet today, a milagro yesterday; a 21st-century holographic sticker, a late-19th-century Victorian scrap — have little-to-no monetary worth. Yet, their cherished personal value can be immeasurable. *Sonoran Borders* is the story of simple objects and the friendship that developed between the women who made them.

While the objects in this book date back more than a century, the story itself has been ruminating for only a decade or so. What began as an idea for a simple child's book with quaint illustrations somehow morphed into a rather melancholy piece of historical fiction. Then the story took a turn toward a useful book that blended aspects of the above with projects for needlework enthusiasts as well as young hands that may be ready to try handwork projects.

Two unrelated and seemingly random happenings set the actual book in motion: Present-day friends who independently stumbled upon charming but tattered needlework relics and two other casual acquaintances (now friends) who had the confidence to connect me with Kansas City Star Quilts.

What you now have in your hands is an attempt to honor the meaning and importance of items that long ago were relegated to dusty attics, boxes destined for charity bazaars or even worse, the trash bin. Ideally, each of us takes time in our busy lives to slow down long enough to create tiny treasures for our family and friends to enjoy. A handwritten letter or a token made from fabric scraps certainly can bring joy that lasts beyond the moment. As I type this, I'm gazing at a paper scene a friend created for me as a belated Christmas and Valentine's Day gift (yes, tardy is okay when the giver is sincere). In it, she deems me a *sampler maker.* I was humbled and touched to have my creativity recognized and appreciated.

It addition to being a *sampler maker,* though, I like to think of myself as a *peacemaker,* which is another goal of this endeavor. Those of us who love fabric and quilts and samplers truly do appreciate the peace and harmony found in a piece of fabric, and the resulting serendipity when that fabric melds with needle and thread to create a design. There is — and always has been — a sense that all is well when we are tucked under that age-old quilt or well-worn blanket, despite the chaos that may reign right outside our bedroom window.

While the choice of *Sonoran Borders* as the title of this book is not intended as a political commentary, the name is not without meaning. Delightful borders surround the two samplers that inspired the title. The Sonoran Desert is also where the story's main characters, Emily and Feliciana, meet. The Sonoran Desert is a place of contrasts: carpeted with delicate filaree one season, parched and dry the next. Its beauty is a conundrum of harsh hills dotted with vibrant saguaro blossoms. Perhaps the only feature more complex than the landscape is its history, home to centuries of unrest dotted by moments of peace. Yet, this is where our story opens and where two girls from different cultures find peace through a shared passion for needle and thread.

WHAT IS A SAMPLER?

While many readers are familiar with antique needlework samplers, the art form may be unfamiliar to others. In the third edition of *Chats on Old Lace and Needlework* (published in 1919), author Mrs. Lowes said, "A 'sampler' is an example or a sample of the worker's skill and cleverness in design and stitching." This

simple definition takes in the basic characteristics of this needlework endeavor that has existed for centuries.

Then there is the 19th-century verse titled, "Simile":

When every letter with judgment is placed
Exactly proportioned and prettily placed
A sampler resembles an elegant mind
Whose passions by reason subdued and refined
Moves only in lives of affection and duty
Reflecting a picture of order and beauty

Two things the needle and the book we find
Serve to accomplish all the female kind
The shining needle draws the fine spun thread
Bedecks the person and adorns the head.

Since neatness gives the charms that all commends,
The needle is the housewife's choicest friend.
    — Source unknown

The humble needle is referenced in many literary works, including the words of Samuel Woodworth:

The bright little needle — the swift flying needle, the needle directed by beauty and art.

And Shakespeare's description: *So delicate with her needle.*

May every stitch you take with needle and thread be a pleasant one. ✕

This bead-work sampler was made by the great-great-great grandmother of antiques dealer, Linda Schwab. Fortuitously, the piece and its history made their way back to the desert Southwest. When Linda offered it for sale, she had no idea the eventual owner would live practically next door in the Arizona desert. Motifs in the incredibly fine bead work (20 to the inch, sewn to 40-ct linen) exhibit characteristics typical of Mexican samplers. Its maker was Laura Pauline Lilly, born in Texas on May 17, 1878, the third child in a family of three girls and one boy.

While she was young, the border changed and their home town became the property of Mexico. Although the family no longer lived in the U.S., they were still considered citizens. In 1903, Pauline moved to Washington, D.C., and married William Simpson. The couple traveled to Mexico throughout their lives collecting pottery pitchers. They had one daughter, Laura, who died in 1941. Her only child had two boys, the youngest being the father of Linda Schwab.

The central motifs of this sampler are cross stitch over two threads of tightly woven 42-ct linen. Motifs on the three completed sides are worked with multi-colored beads. As is typical of many samplers made in the region, the back is composed of neatly executed vertical stitches. The deer motif inspired projects in Sonoran Borders.

The entire sampler is pictured on page 34 and close-ups are on pages 7 and 35.

CHAPTER 1

Down from the Attic

A joy shared is a joy doubled.

—Goethe

The sound of the creaking stairs warmed Feliciana's heart. She had climbed each of the 23 steps countless times throughout her life — beginning as a teen, escaping chores or study or laborious visits from doting neighbors and well-intentioned relatives. Through the beveled glass in the carefully leaded windows, she could glimpse the bay or the clouds or even imagine she were back on the ranch in Sonora where she spent her early years. Later, the attic brought a sense of order to a chaotic life because it was there that she stored neatly folded blankets, sweaters and linens, and stacks of books, letters and papers. She could not bear to part with tattered books and torn linens, unless, of course, she could find a loving home for them.

Collection of Jeremy Rowe Vintage Photography, vintagephoto.com

"Abuela, Abuela," Anna called, "look what I found hidden inside a suitcase deep within a large painted trunk in the attic. Aren't they so beautiful?"

Feliciana had not been in the attic since the early days of World War II, six years of chaos and devastation that thankfully had ended with a peace treaty two years ago. She remembered that last trek up the steps. She had just received an unexpected parcel from Tucson and wanted to tuck it away for safekeeping. A terse note accompanied its contents. The writer could not have known the significance of these objects: "Moved into home and found this box in a closet. Former owner deceased and had no relatives. Did not want to discard contents and this name and address was on every envelope. We hope you will know what to do. Kind regards, Mr. and Mrs. Ramon Rivera."

Now Feliciana was curious about the treasure her nine-year-old granddaughter had unearthed. The trunk was one of few material remnants from her family's journey north from Mexico nearly 60 years ago. She smiled as Anna jumped into her lap, bringing her huge dimples and the gentle scent of just-washed hair.

Simply delightful, she thought, simply delightful.

The child's enthusiasm spilled into every breath she took, every word she uttered. Oblivious to the strains of the day, Anna brought much needed levity to the Martinez Delgado household where life seemed to

Collection of Jeremy Rowe Vintage Photography, vintagephoto.com

tumble downward ever since the Great Earthquake and Fire of 1906.

"Look, Abuela! Look! These are so pretty. Do you see the little girl sewn into the fabric?"

With that, Anna jumped from the chair, twirled in a circle and posed like the girl sewn on the fabric, even pretending to carry a flower in one hand and a basket in the other.

"Doesn't she look just like me? Do you think I could take the sewing pictures to my room and tack them to the wall? I love the small dogs and the huge red birds. There, see the giant pot of orange flowers and the tiny blue birds? Are they yours? Wherever did you get these?"

Feliciana's gnarled fingers ran across the coarse linen, the very touch transporting her to the vast desert where these simple girlhood embroideries came to be. She was perhaps a few years older than Anna when she and Emily created these "sewing pictures" — an apt description of the little samplers stitched in the late 1800s by two unlikely friends.

"Well, mi angelita, I did not exactly 'get' these little samplers, I made them, with the help of a dear, dear friend."

"You mean you did all this sewing with your own hands and everything? Oh they are so wonderful! And your friend — I didn't know that grandmothers had friends."

"Strange, I know," Feliciana chuckled, recalling her childhood and similar feelings she once had about her elders — los viejos. "Let me tell you about this particular friend of mine. Her name was Emily Catherine and she lived with her mother in Tucson, Arizona."

"Is that far from the Bay, Abuela?"

"Oh my goodness, yes, dear. It is in a very hot desert much like our family's homeland."

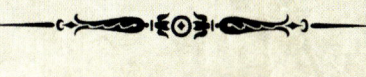

This undated antique inspired the For My Friend by Feliciana *sampler.*

"But why did your friend live so far away?"

"Because that is where her family settled. How I longed to remain amongst the cactus and sagebrush, but it wasn't to be."

"Why?"

"The paths of our families simply did not permit that. Yet, through many years of correspondence, Emily and I managed to develop and maintain a friendship beyond compare."

Anna settled in for a story that would chronicle two lifetimes …

To make *For My Friend by Feliciana*, see page 48.

CHAPTER 2

Once Upon a Sonoran Desert Morn

True friend, my wellspring in the wilderness.

—George Eliot
(pen name of Mary Anne Evans)

FROM FELICIANA MARTINEZ:

Once upon a Sonoran desert morn we met, Emily Catherine Alexander's moss green eyes forever embedded in my mind. In the first days of our friendship, we could talk only with our eyes — hers drenched in pain and tears. I spoke no English, she no Spanish, but words would have done little, if anything, to heal her agony. Sometimes steady, other times shaking, her hands were almost always occupied by needle and thread. These simple objects alone were her comfort. Who would imagine that such commonplace instruments as needle and thread, pen and paper could forge a life-long friendship?

Oh, but I am getting ahead of myself. She was such a precious friend, perhaps one I never would have had were it not for the anguish she endured during those tender first days we shared in the lacy shade of a lone palo verde tree along the Santa Cruz River.

Much to the relief of my father and mother, few distractions and certainly no disasters had interrupted our journey north from Magdalena, Sonora. We had been traveling for several days when we noticed smoke rising from a camp near the river. Ever cautious along the arduous route where potential perils lurked behind mountains and around bends, several of the men rode ahead to assess the situation. What they found shook even the toughest of ranchers: a wounded girl reclined in the back of a wagon, her distorted leg swollen nearly twice its usual size.

They rode back, encouraging my mother to locate her teas and herbs to treat the injured girl. She asked me to accompany her, my task being to hold the girl's hand. I did not want to go.

Tears had been my companion along the trail, for I was not keen about leaving the only home I had ever

Collection of Jeremy Rowe Vintage Photography, vintagephoto.com

known. The last thing I wanted to do at the moment was to help with chores. My mother, however, reminded me of our duty to assist those in need, recalling the wounded birds we brought home for care. I rode behind Father on a horse, carrying water and some supplies. Mother rode alone. Everyone else followed at a slow pace.

Despite the silence, tension cloaked the travelers' camp. I dismounted, avoiding the girl's festering leg and gazing immediately at her eyes. We noticed one another's cultural differences right away, but we did not share these initial observations for many years. We sensed our parents' trepidation, yet we felt no fear. She managed a weak smile, I a grin, for something inside told me cheer is what this girl needed most of all. Perhaps these were nervous smiles, not knowing what else to do.

Through gestures and drawings on Emily's chalkboard, our mothers were able to communicate the particulars of the mishap. Apparently she was riding her favorite horse alongside the wagon when a rattlesnake spooked the animal, sending it into a bucking fit. Thrown from the horse, Emily landed between a huge cactus and a boulder, crushing and mangling her thorn-embedded leg.

Emily floated in and out of consciousness, wincing but never crying out, in what must have been a dreadful pain. Once treated, her injury was hidden under the delicate flowers printed on her dress or beneath a patchwork quilt fashioned from fabric scraps. Mother treated it with poultices many times during the ensuing weeks.

We had not planned this diversion, and many times I wished only that we could return home and not continue our trek north. Some members of our party did move forward, but my family and a few others remained until Emily's fever broke.

For days Emily lay in her makeshift bed attempting to copy images from a beautiful sampler her grandmother had embroidered many years before we met. I recalled a similar treasure that my abuela had made with vibrant and beautiful silk threads. It remained home in Mexico with the rest of the family. The spectacular crimson and deep blues of Abuela's sampler were far different than the muted shades in the sampler Emily's grandmother had created. Yet as dissimilar as they were, the needlework also possessed distinct common traits.

Certainly our ancestors lived far from one another, yet each had created her own needlework to serve as a pattern displaying the alphabet or words, and hand-stitched pictures — for not even photographs had been invented all those years ago. The carefully-formed fabric images produced records and stories of our ancestors' lives, stitched onto pieces of linen that became our introduction to one another.

During those few weeks in the desert, I sat with Emily as she discovered desert sunsets. Her eyes widened each evening as she breathed in the very essence of our surroundings. The day's giant fiery orb eased its way down into the western sky, taking with it kernels of the day and the last bits of blue sky — cielo azul. We shared our experiences each as best we could in our own languages. As we watched, enraptured by the light dancing on the desert, peach gave way to lavender and then purple, until blackness eventually enveloped our campsite. Days of worry and tears faded into the dark of night, blending with tunes from my brother's fiddle. Our perennial perch was the back of Emily's wagon, because at that point her body remained frail from the infection. Her mind, forever active, asking questions by drawing delightful figures on her chalkboard while asking, "¿Cómo se dice?" She was particularly delighted just to repeat my name, "Feliciana Lucia Martinez, my friend."

Emily was as eager to learn Spanish as I English, for her family was bound for Tucson, where she, her mother and brother would reside. Her father was already in a place called Fort Apache, an outpost in the mountains of Arizona Territory, where he was responsible for securing the health and welfare of the animals. She was excited for the day her family could be reunited. ✕

To make *For My Friend by Emily*, see page 52.

CHAPTER 3

Up from Magdalena

Nothing makes the earth seem so spacious as to have friends at a distance.

—Henry David Thoreau

Looking back, I now understand why my parents chose to venture forth from, what seemed to me, a most cozy, comfortable and sprawling ranch. The hills, our corrals and vast pastures were filled with cattle, such docile animals that provided much of my family's livelihood. Some were milk cows, others were range cattle. I cannot be certain, but I do believe the animal pictured in the little sampler made by my Tía Maria may be a Jersey, a breed that was imported across the Atlantic from the Jersey Isles. The cows that lived close to the hacienda lounged under the trees, forever munching feed and chewing their cud as they took cover from the blazing afternoon sun. Perhaps it is the palo verde tree she pictured in her sampler.

I remember looking at it, recalling the pump house she captured with needle and thread. It stood next to her home, just down the lane from ours. And she even stitched the small hand-pump in the yard where we fetched water for the animals. Little birds often visited to take baths and get a drink. I remember the dogs and roosters that occupied our ranch, and, yes, occasional Coues deer that strayed into the pastures, feasting upon whatever crop was growing at the time — sometimes wheat, other times maize or sorghum.

Many members of our family remained at our tranquil ranch, located on the fringes of a rather disorderly area plagued by tension and unrest related to political power and land ownership. My own grandmother cried as she and the aunts helped us pack the trunk and

the precious few possessions that could be stowed in our wagons. For days, we prepared food and water for our travels across the border. My father believed that moving to the city was necessary for the well-being of our family and also for the opportunity to secure work. He knew of men who'd found jobs in the mines and on the railroad, but he eventually found employment with a steamship company.

Leaving home caused great pain for all of us. I did not know what to feel. When I closed my eyes at night, memories swam across the backs of my eyelids like a rolling tide. I woke up to a tear-stained pillow, not understanding why we had to leave. What I could not know then — for children need not concern themselves with the woes of the world — is that great turmoil

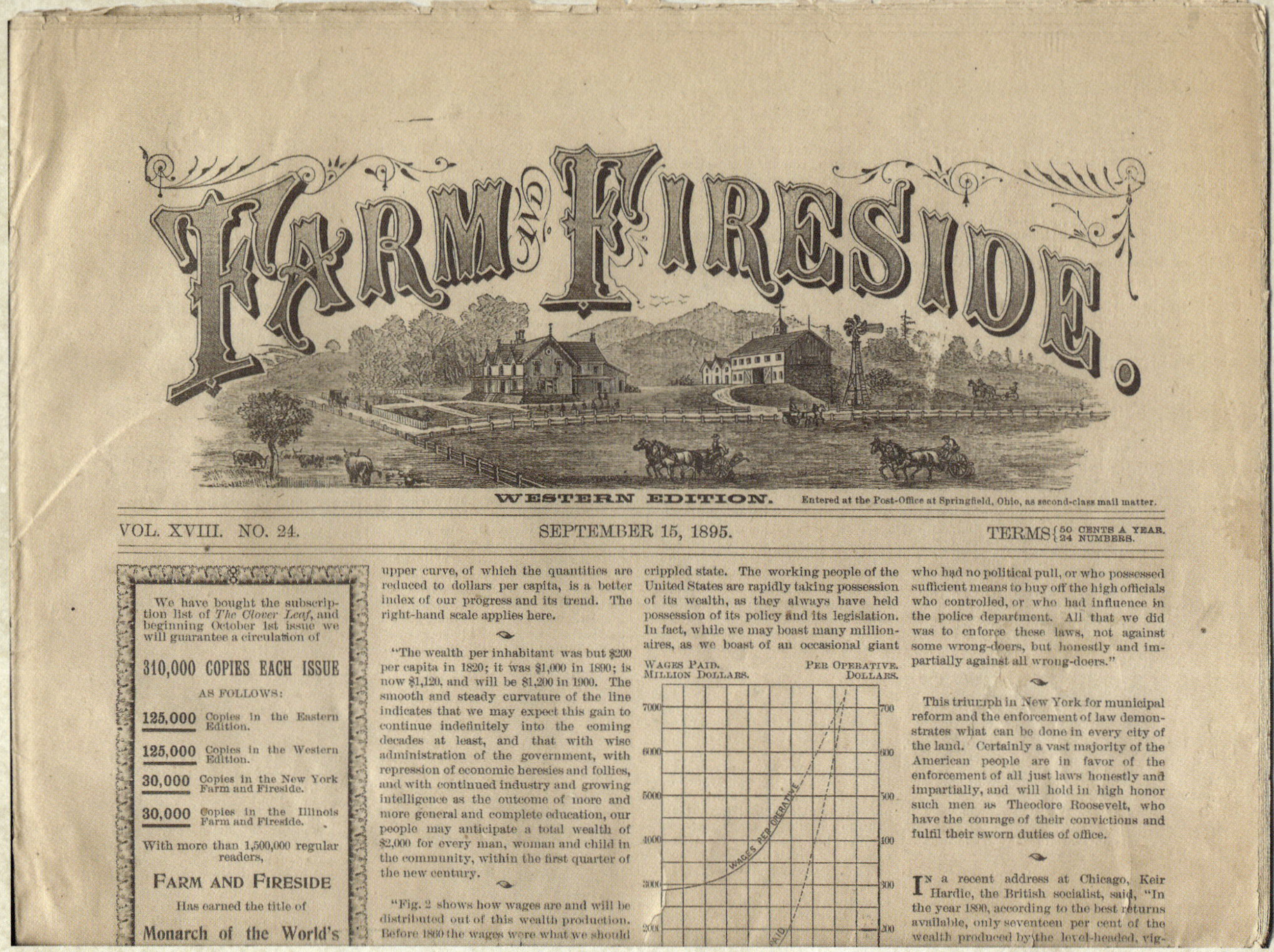

Farm and Fireside.

WESTERN EDITION. Entered at the Post-Office at Springfield, Ohio, as second-class mail matter.

VOL. XVIII. NO. 24.   SEPTEMBER 15, 1895.   TERMS {50 CENTS A YEAR. 24 NUMBERS.

We have bought the subscription list of *The Clover Leaf*, and beginning October 1st issue we will guarantee a circulation of

310,000 COPIES EACH ISSUE

AS FOLLOWS:

125,000 Copies in the Eastern Edition.
125,000 Copies in the Western Edition.
30,000 Copies in the New York Farm and Fireside.
30,000 Copies in the Illinois Farm and Fireside.

With more than 1,500,000 regular readers,

FARM AND FIRESIDE

Has earned the title of

Monarch of the World's

---

actually waged in our beloved homeland. The disputes were many and involved myriad well-intentioned and passionate people — President Porfirio Diaz, Cajeme, Carlos Ortiz and General Luis Torres, to name a few — seeking control for their causes: independence, economic well-being, land ownership. Some were loyal to the official government of Mexico, others to the native Yaqui Indians. Still others were content to spend their lives oblivious to the unrest. This, I believe, is how our relatives preferred to go about their days.

Our small family of six left Sonora, along with three or four other families, just after uprisings and skirmishes took place not far from our home. We were not personally troubled by the chaos, but I do recall the hushed voices of adults talking about animals being confiscated, towns being occupied and battles being fought. Both soldiers and innocent people were killed. Eventually, though, we learned through letters from family and newspaper reports, that an official peace treaty was signed. Nonetheless, unrest reigned near the ranch, and my parents maintained until their deaths that our move to San Francisco was for the best. ✕

To make *Sonoran Borders Sampler*, see page 56.

CHAPTER 4

Be of Comfort, One to Another

Backward, turn backward,
*   O Time in your flight,*
Make me a child again, just for to-night…
Backward, flow backward,
*   O tide of the years!*
I am so weary of toil and tears…

> —From "Rock Me to Sleep, Mother"
> by Elizabeth Akers Allen, 1882

Many months, or perhaps a year, had passed before I truly understood why Emily and her family were in the Arizona desert. During those days in the desert, we did manage to teach one another words and phrases, as well as sharing a love of needle and thread, but we knew little to nothing else about our families, our homes, our friends or our histories. Those particulars just did not have a place when Emily was struggling to survive, nor were our skills in one another's languages sufficient to share the exacting details that accompanied our childhood years.

Emily and her traveling companions had nearly completed their long journey from Missouri to Tucson. My family, on the other hand — y por otro lado — still needed to make their way along the Santa Cruz River, up to Maricopa Wells, then over to Fort Yuma and on to San Diego where we would board a ship bound for San Francisco.

Parting ways brought unexpected emotion to both of us. Never before and never again did I experience such an immediate bond with another friend. Our tearful goodbyes gave way to arduous travel that eventually led to new surroundings.

Once in our new home, my sisters, brother and I were enrolled in school and started to learn English. I felt quite accomplished when I was able to write my first letter using English words to my new friend, Emily. Although this was many months after our initial meeting in the desert, I would not rest until I found a way to post my greetings to Emily and to inquire about her recovery. My father provided an envelope. Inside I tucked a few drawings fashioned after my aunt's sampler, as well as my letter. I simply addressed the envelope: Miss Emily Catherine Alexander, Tucson, Arizona Territory.

Some months later, I received an eloquent response, detailing the continued healing of her leg and the sad news that her father had died of consumption while at Fort Apache. Despite this loss, Emily's mother decided to remain in Tucson where the children attended school and helped with the boarding house her mother

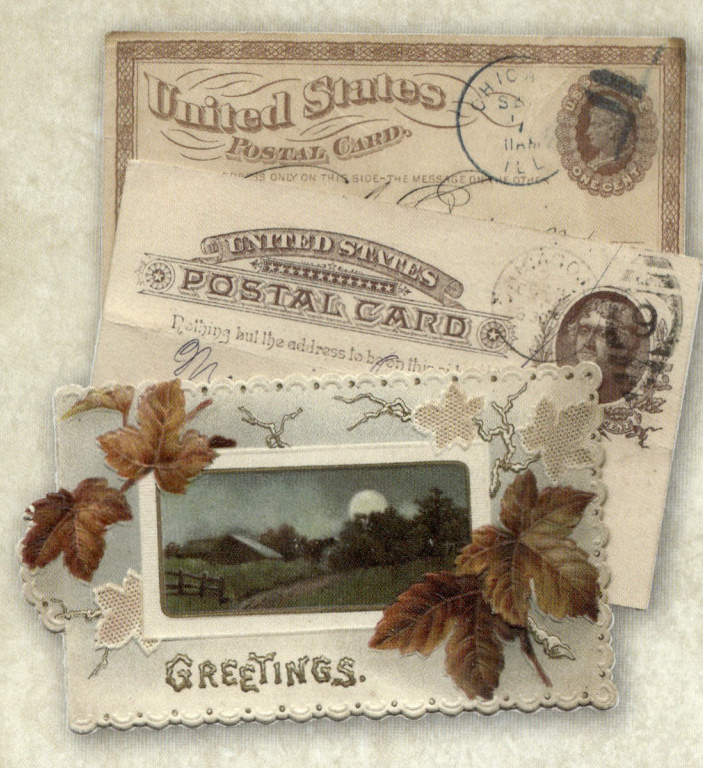

operated. Much to my delight, Emily's correspondence included an elongated emery to store sewing needles that she had fashioned from a scrap of velvet upholstery. She wrote of the scarcity of needles, as the general store had run out of some items and weeks may pass before the stock could be replenished. Emily said she stored her precious needles in an old emery that belonged to her mother.

Although Emily was learning some conversational Spanish, she chose to write in her native English, creating images that transported me to the Delaware seacoast where she lived before her family moved to Missouri.

I, Emily Catherine Alexander, born in 1885 in Lewes, Delaware, have a story to tell, if only I could pen a tale as enchanting as the ones I have read in Gulliver's Travels. *My journey is far from being as spectacular as Gulliver's land and sea escapades, but is an adventure that has taken me from my birthplace by the sea to*

Collection of Jeremy Rowe Vintage Photography, vintagephoto.com

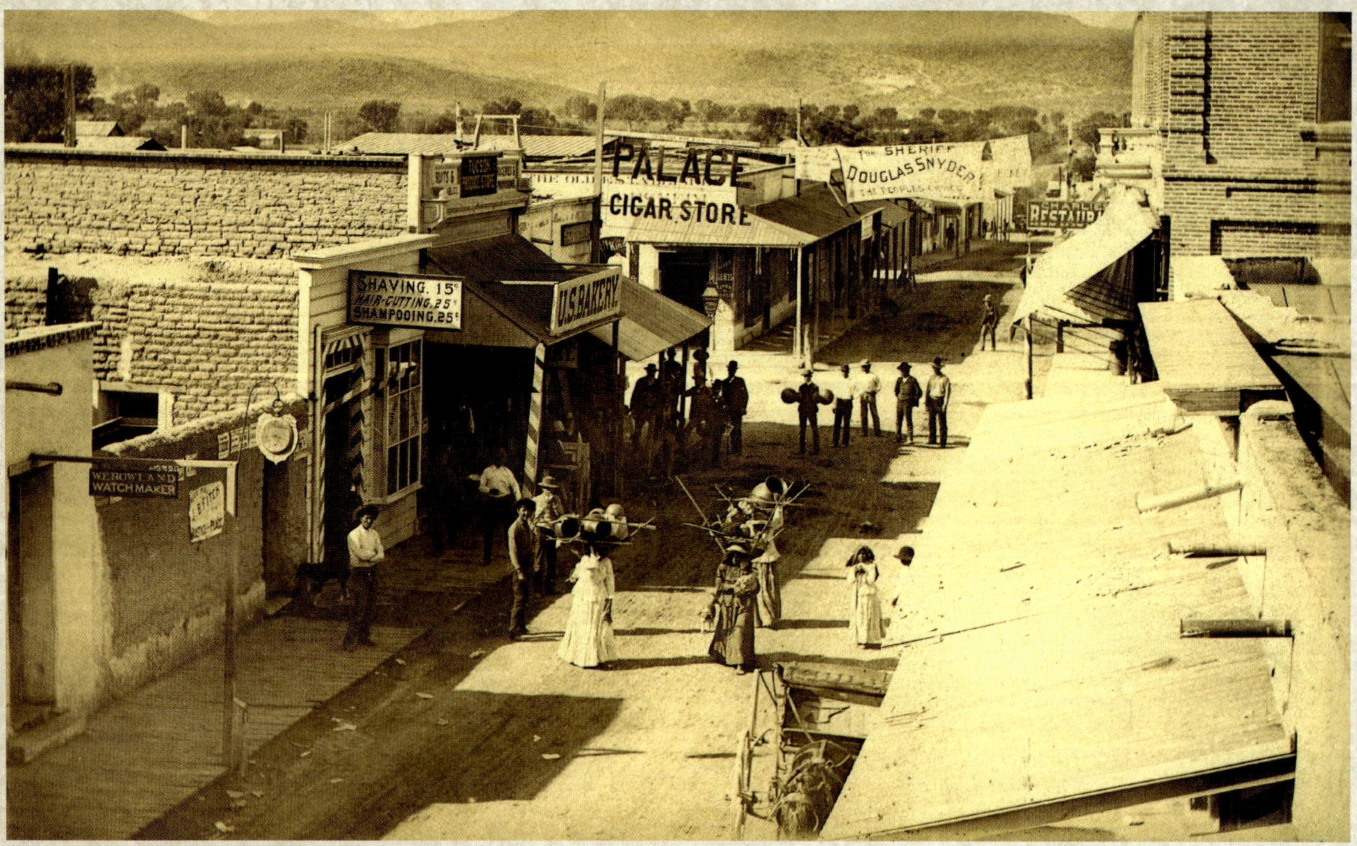

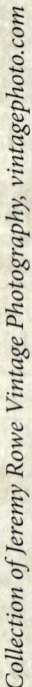

the budding town of Independence, Missouri, and on to a vast and curious desert in a place called Arizona Territory. My story is plain, but it is true. It is humble, but full of love. It is simple, but it is sincere. I had neither the skill nor the time to record our adventures from Lewes to Independence. My father's trade as a veterinary surgeon is what prompted each of our moves through harsh weather, whipping winds, freezing nights and scorching sun. I left Independence, an able-bodied girl, expecting to help mother settle into our boarding house in Tucson. Alas, a careless moment led to the crushing of my right leg, so now I must transfer my energy from my once-strong leg to my hands, so that I may record with my pen and with my needle that which we are enduring. My art is my salvation from the pain that plagues my leg. I think I should go mad were it not for my pen and ink, needle and thread.

So, this is where our paths crossed, at a moment when we had nothing but time to watch as a full moon rose. We counted the stars — uno, dos, tres — one, two three. In her letters, Emily expressed gratitude that my mother had remedies with healing properties, remedies passed on by her mother and her mother's mother. She only wished such a cure had existed for her father's consumption. Certainly Emily never complained, yet she openly lamented the lack of conveniences she had come to appreciate in Independence.

At the same time, my life was only beginning to adjust to the conveniences of a growing city. My heart, however, yearned to be back in the desert, to experience its blessed silence. "Will a time come," she asked, "when there is no grief, no suffering, no sadness?" She then closed her five-page letter encouraging me to "proceed with wisdom, courage and grace."

That is, in fact, what we did. Even though our families' lives were dismantled in those early days, we slowly rebuilt and renovated our relationships. ✕

To make *Velvet Scrap Emery and Pincushion,* **see page 60.**

Chapter 5

Direct from My Loving Hands

May I delight in doing good,
In justice, peace and gratitude.

—19th-century sampler verse

With great fondness I recall the encouraging words Emily and I exchanged. We never knew when the other's post box would contain correspondence, but we were certain our communications would continue. Even my mother smiled when crisp white paper displaying joyful hands clasped in friendship dropped from a dingy and tattered envelope.

Inside was a pristine and most welcome letter accompanying the stitched card. It read, "Your toil is not in vain, dearest Feliciana, for you, like your mother, are the vision of an industrious and virtuous woman whose efforts reflect what is good and right in this world."

How those few words of encouragement buoyed our spirits. This particular letter arrived sometime between the Great Earthquake of 1906 and the Spanish Influenza outbreak about 12 years later. I cannot read the date, but if I recall correctly, Emily was responding to news of the sleepless nights and excruciating tasks that followed the quake and resulting fire. I had written to her detailing the move from our home to a park where we resided for weeks with hundreds of other families. Those of us who were able cared for the injured and sick. I cannot say which was more terrifying — the physical calamity or the fear. ¡Persevera en todo!

We tried, oh we tried so very hard, not to focus on what had occurred and what could happen, especially with the devastation that surrounded us. We

by Arizona's statehood, but also with enfranchisement for Emily, her mother and all women in the nation's newest state.

Sharing these experiences on paper helped both Emily and me to move through the trials. Weeks and months often passed before our letters reached their destination, allowing us time for our emotions to settle and wounds to heal. Perhaps this was the purpose for our paths to cross. I have often pondered our chance meeting in the desert. Rather than fading, though, our friendship flourished and blossomed like the delicate flowers these hands proffer. It is no wonder they were immortalized in paper, thread and even a bronze button. We encouraged and restored one another, resulting in an ongoing renewal that came from simple and honest support. Much effort was directed at survival and simply safeguarding the well-being of our families.

Emily ended one of her letters from this time: "Would that I could send you an image or an essay as vibrant as the setting sun here in the great desert surrounding Tucson. Rather, I extend these flowers of friendship." ✕

were awakened early that fateful morning by great trembling, followed by screams and crashing. Many buildings tumbled while others remained intact with windows and chimneys blown out. Fire then ravaged the city for three days, as steam engines attempted to put out what fires they could. Although more than a dozen years had passed, our city had finally recovered from this disaster when World War I and the Spanish Influenza broke out. All these years later, the tragedies somehow blend in my mind, like the smoke that rose from all sections of our beloved city, burning our eyes and clouding our vision for many days. I pray that such a calamity never befalls my grandchildren. My throat tightens, and I can almost taste this recollection of pain and suffering.

But, we had no choice in the moment. We went to work, celebrated baptisms, marriages and quinceañeras, buried the dead, went back to work and laughed at jokes. Often they were just plain silly, but true mirthful laughter was good for our souls. During that time, we rallied with women throughout the great State of California to earn the right to vote. Our 1911 victory was followed the next year not only

To make *From My Loving Hands*, see page 62.

CHAPTER 6

On Education and Related Matters

One of our great pleasures over the years was swapping verses on a variety of topics, including education. These are some I have committed to memory:

There is nothing of so much worth
As a mind well instructed.

By observing the truth you will command esteem
And secure your own peace.

To you my kind parents this work I present
And hope it will please you and give you content.
and merit your further kind favor.

Both Emily and I were eager to begin our schooling when we arrived at our new homes. Each of us found our schools far different than what we had experienced before our westward journeys. I learned not only the English language, but also Greek and mathematics.

Emily also studied mathematics, but, despite her wishes, learned little Spanish in the classroom. Rather, she picked up a command of the language through practical conversation and our correspondence. In Missouri, her studies included needlework and sewing; in Tucson, sewing became a leisure pursuit. I had the good fortune of finding an embroidery room in San Francisco where new techniques and fibers were introduced.

Emily's enthusiasm for learning led her to continue her formal education toward teacher training so she, too, could instruct young and eager minds. My passion for numbers permitted me to assist my family in our import business, a trade my father was so proud to develop after years working on the steam ships. Our education was simple and useful, but the skills we procured were so enduring. Still today, I appreciate the attention devoted to developing beautiful handwriting and studying classic art.

My walk to school afforded the opportunity to pass by beautiful flowers during the spring and early summer months. Oh how I longed to share with my friend in Tucson the jasmine's sweet scent or a garland fashioned from brilliant camellias growing on the verdant bushes. Although this could not be, I did send my friend in the desert a tiny flower-laden pin cushion and she returned a note of gratitude accompanied by a whimsical peacock to remind me of the many varieties of birds that used to populate our farmyard. Once we moved to the city, the only peacocks I saw were in public gardens and aviaries or picture books.

Although many miles and our different life paths separated us, together we managed to post messages that helped us learn about our passions, our dignity, and our place and meaning in the world. I told her how despite its grand buildings, natural beauty and tremendous opportunities, the city still shouldered a gray emptiness. When I expressed my longing for the familiar desert scenes and smells, Emily wrote back explaining that even though I recalled its splendor, she experienced claustrophobia amidst the desert's vastness, trapped by a leg that limited her mobility and an ailing mother who needed constant care. We garnered strength for the journey through our letters.

To make *Peacock Pincushion*,
see page 64.

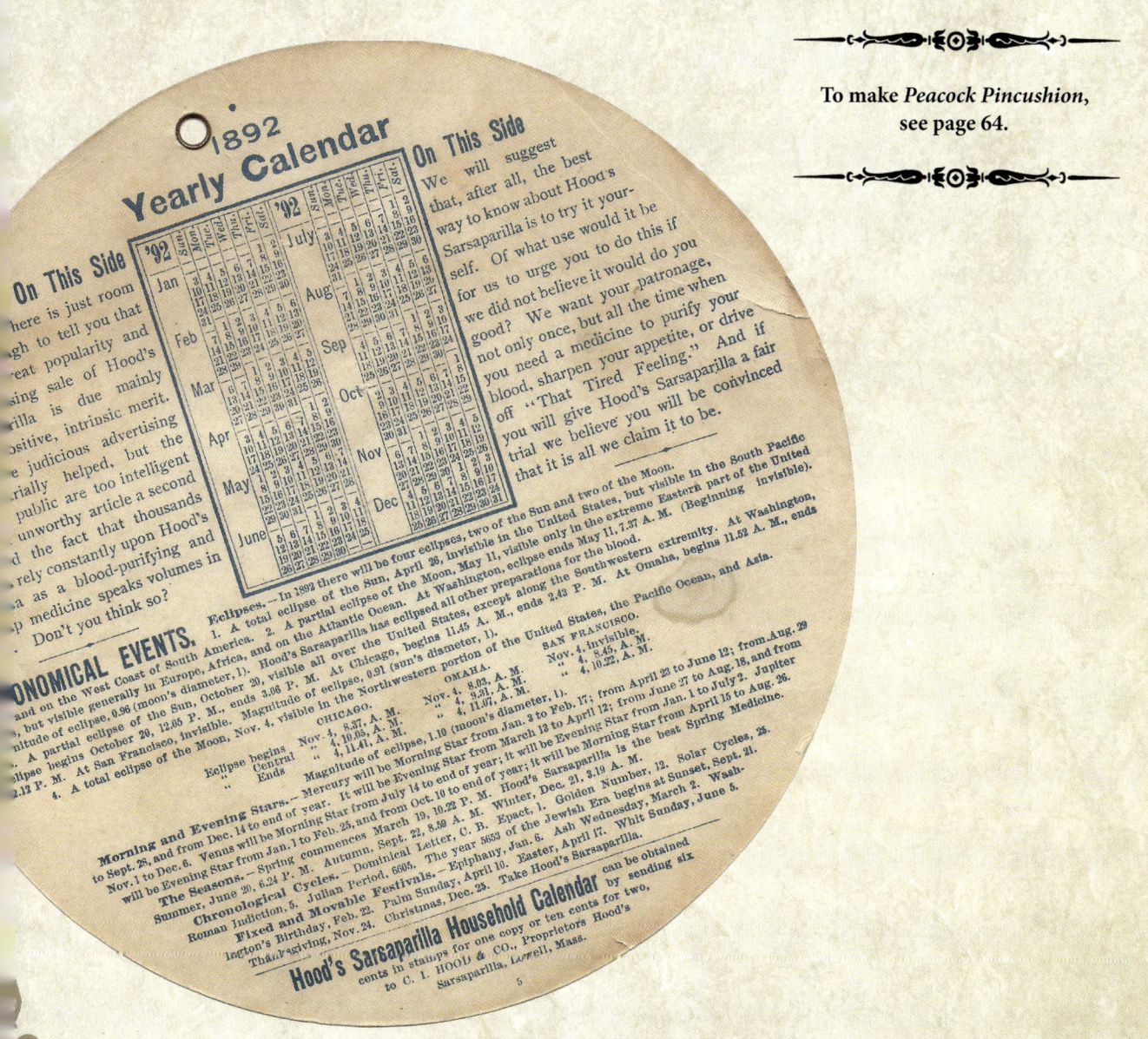

CHAPTER 7

A Testament to Family, Friendship and Food

*Friendship is a glorious melody whose
beauty increases with the passage of time.*

—Jane Pierre

Your sweet friendship is a blessing.

—Source unknown

*Accept dear parents this tribute due
For favors conferred on me by you
And may my latest actions show
I was not unworthy of the care you
    now bestow.*

—19th-century sampler verse

Somehow, from an early age, Emily and I both knew that our loyalty was first to our families — as well as our pleasure. Perhaps this fundamental belief is what created the bond of friendship that grew from our brief encounter in the desert Southwest so many years ago. As silly as it sounds, from that first glimpse of a full moon rising in the east on an early April night, we shared a fascination with the notion that, despite the miles separating us, our hearts could be one as we glanced at the same moon rising as it cycled through its predictable phases. Little else in life is as predictable.

Perhaps, though, this is how it should be. Were we to know and understand each day's trials and joys,

we may never venture from the comfort of our beds or step outside our front doors. Our beloved Sunday gatherings were a welcome respite from the toil and trepidation that existed. Burdens lifted, we looked only to the blessings around the table each week. Thoughtfully and carefully prepared, our meals did so much more than fill our stomachs. We enjoyed albondigas or menudo, green corn tamales, always a fresh fish — pescado fresco — and enchiladas de pollo. And the desserts — rich flan or dulce de leche, both served with generous portions of apricots or strawberries — filled the wooden sideboard that sat next to the hearth. Cooking often commenced the day before, with the freshest of ingredients — herbs and vegetables, meats and fruits — stocking the pantry and ice box (its invention a real saving grace) even when times were lean.

After dinner one Sunday night, I recall walking outside with my mother and sharing with her my little ritual about the moon. She was so pleased to hear about this practice, because she said the moon brought her a similar comfort as she, too, longed sometimes to be home with our relatives.

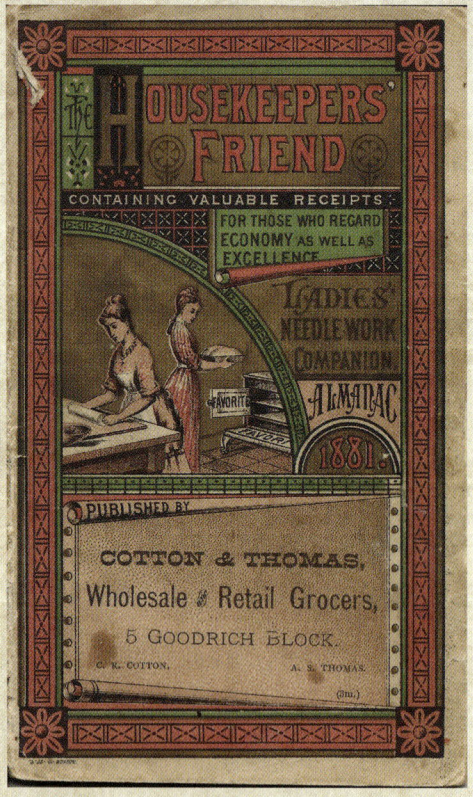

Duty called us back to the kitchen that evening and we came back down to earth and focused on the task at hand. The practical nature of our lives taught us at a young age to appreciate the day that was in front of us — to profit from the past and hope for the future, but to focus our attention on the present. Even when troubles assaulted our patience and threatened our very survival, we never questioned the importance of belonging to and believing in one another.

Each of our families had our own distressing and dramatic realities. I remember taking milagros to the church where we asked for mercy upon the suffering. Small metal tokens represented Papa's ailing back or the food we sometimes needed to fill our pantry. We lit candles and prayed for deliverance from pain and hard times. We also gave thanks for that which was right and good in our lives. Suffering certainly has meaning and value, although at times we had difficulty seeing its merits.

As the years passed, we learned to look back with joy upon our homeland and those who went before us who left a rich legacy. We came to appreciate the restorative power of food and rest and quiet. Nothing could take away these memories held deep inside. Emily and I did not let our hearts grow hard; rather, we continued sending small tokens of great regard. I remember that many years had passed when I pieced this simple table mat for Emily. I was taking my last stitches in front of the radio when President Coolidge gave the first presidential broadcast in 1923. Emily had just gone back to teaching after her mother died. No one could fill her mother's place at the table, but a gift from a friend reminded Emily that someone cared. ✕

To make *Deer to My Hearts* Table Mat, see page 66.

CHAPTER 8

Just a Little Kindness Makes the World a Better Place

Smile upon a stranger.

—Folk saying

Perhaps my first awareness of the meaning of kindness to strangers occurred all those years ago along that dusty and long trail up from Mexico. Truly, before that time, I knew little of the world outside our ranch and nearby villages. Family and friends made up our community in Magdalena. Our easy familiarity provided great safety and comfort for a young girl.

My grandmother said, "carry on in joy" — ¡Sigue adelante con alegría! — and "extend kindness to strangers," as we ventured out for the city. Little did we know that shortly into our journey, her simple but sage advice would enkindle a life-long friendship with a girl from a family who had embarked on a similar journey.

Collection of Jeremy Rowe Vintage Photography, vintagephoto.com

Over those years, as we made San Francisco our home, we experienced countless opportunities for kindness. Traveling up and down the seacoast on steamships, my father was forever befriending strangers. Sometimes we welcomed them into our home for dinner, other times for an extended stay. When I entered school in the city, strangers filled the classroom, where I occupied a seat in the far back corner. The rows of wooden desks leading up to the front of the room seemed endless. I hid my initial trepidation behind a tender smile that must have conveyed kindness because, in short order, the smiles led to simple conversations, schoolyard games, and eventually true and lasting friendships.

Simple sewing was part of our curriculum in primary school, and I recall girls bringing fabric scraps, which we traded in order to have a variety of colors for our small notions rollups. The rollup we constructed in school included only fabric scraps, but a few years later, I inserted linen panels in one I'd fashioned at home for Emily, stitching a few motifs from family marking samplers. Inside, I tucked two milagros I thought she would enjoy. A hand and flower adorned the silver charm, while the brass milagro was a girl who reminded me of Emily. Years later she wrote that she wore one on her watch chain while the other was pinned to her classroom bulletin board.

I have always imagined Emily's classroom to be a pleasant place, at times unruly but forever engaging, even capturing students' attention on the hottest of desert days. She once described the maps — collected from all corners of the world — that decorated the classroom walls. Many maps were donated by strangers who passed through Tucson or with whom Emily had corresponded with over the years. I am certain she was the type of teacher who tempered discipline with kindness in an attempt to cultivate curiosity and encourage learning. ✕

To make *Simple Sewing Rollup*, see page 70.

CHAPTER 9
All That's Old is New Again

The best mirror is an old friend.

—Spanish proverb

Much to my surprise and delight, on a spring day in 1896, a parcel appeared at our door. I remember the year well, because it was the year of my marriage to Hector. He had heard of my friend, Emily, and had even admired her handwork. A simple note tucked inside the hand-made purse read, "Pieces of the past brought together for your future." The inside of the multi-colored purse provided functional space for needle and thread, a small comb, scissors and perhaps a few other personal items. Emily's stitching adorned the outside, where she paired white doves on the front panel with a scene from my homeland on the back.

While joyful, the actual preparation for marriage is amazingly cumbersome, which is why to this day, I treasure the sentiment and simplicity of Emily's thoughtful and very personal wedding gift. She had extracted images from samplers we had made in prior

years and arranged them on the purse, for example, la paloma blanca — the white dove — standing for innocence, tenderness and meekness. As children, we were all of these, longing also to be free like the birds. Because the dove is thought to mate for life, placement of the two doves together represents marital fidelity. The fact that the doves are facing one another shows peace and contentment, which Hector and I shared for nearly 50 years. Nothing, save his death, could separate us. And, while the figural flowers in the doves' mouths likely were not olive leaves, their presence reminded me of Noah's Ark and the biblical story of the dove returning with an olive leaf in its mouth. Perhaps I read too much into these stitches, but I think not. Emily planned every one, including the conjoined hearts. As was the tradition, the guests at our wedding formed a heart around us during our first dance as husband and wife.

On the purse, Emily also rearranged some memories I had recounted and stitched from my life in Magdalena — a beloved cow, dog and bird, all within a landscape scene. My family and I often dreamed of going back to the ranch, but none of us ever left northern California. A part of me always felt connected to that great Sonoran desert, yet my roots were firmly planted and grew in the Bay area. A house, after all, is but a building. A home is where you grow up, raise a family,

and live out your dreams. For me, those dreams took the form of a growing and loving family. When Emily's mother died, her classroom became her family.

I wrote to Emily each time a child came into our lives: Little Hector was born into this world the last day of 1899, the twins, Carlos and Henrietta, in 1902, Javier in 1905, then Maria in 1908. I was never one for keeping a diary, but because Emily saved my letters, the simple pleasures and accomplishments of raising a family are now recorded for the next generation. That generation includes 11 grandchildren, and now two great-grandchildren.

Although my friend never married nor revealed the reason for this choice, she certainly shared and rejoiced in our happiness, always understanding and empathizing with the situations posed in our correspondence. What a joy to have a friend whose affection was unconditional! She once told me that rather than viewing her permanent limp as a handicap, she looked upon it as a reminder of the bond we established. ✕

To make *Las Palomas Blancas Purse*, see page 74.

CHAPTER 10

The Story of My Life is Wrapped in These Threads

*With mirth and laughter let
old wrinkles come.*

—William Shakespeare

As Feliciana held the purse, she looked down at the shadows created by furrows in her hands. Skin and vein tributaries led to knotty knuckles tipped with petite white nails. How those hands had changed over the years! They reminded her of the times when water was so scarce that hand washing was more a luxury than a necessity. Her youthful hands wrote letters, stitched gifts, played games, cradled babies and cooked meals. In recent years, they sat folded in her lap, too tired to take on the tasks that once had brought her so much pleasure. She looked, too, at the gold band she had not removed in more than 50 years.

Hector died while Juan was off at war. Hector never saw the medals and ribbons that decorated his oldest grandson's uniform or the smiles now on his youngest granddaughter's face.

"Ours was a good life though," she said to no one and everyone, "blessed with a loving family and many friends."

"What, Abuela?" Anna asked.

Feliciana removed a small silver token from a pocket in the purse. A delicate beaded edge bordered the central turtledoves.

"For you," she said, gently placing the disc in Anna's soft, young hands.

"My hope, dear Anna, is that sharing these memories and small treasures will help you understand and appreciate pieces of my past as you venture into a hope-filled future. Certainly you may tack the sampler picture to your wall. Its beauty is meant to be celebrated, not buried deep inside a chest of memories. Perhaps one day, your father will make a frame for it." ✕

To make *Perforated Paper Pieces*, see page 84.

1979
Anna's Epilogue

Abuela died shortly after my wedding in 1958. She never made it back to the desert, but I promised I would visit there one day. Thankfully that day came when I made a trip to see my son who was accepted into the agriculture program at the University of Arizona in Tucson. We drove deep into the Santa Catalina Mountains where, on a summer monsoon day, I came to understand her affection for the desert.

Oddly enough, on our way back into town, we stopped at a secondhand store where I found two small, framed alphabets that looked much like those my grandmother and her friend Emily had stitched in their youth. My fascination with these attracted the shopkeeper's attention.

"Take them, dear," he said. "They have been gathering dust for years."

"Oh, but I must pay you something."

"I won't hear of it," he insisted. "No one has paid them any notice. I'm certain they will fare far better in a home than buried on these shelves."

We traded smiles as he wrapped the gift. The alphabets made the trip back to San Francisco with me where they joined the "sewing pictures" my father had framed for me three decades ago. ✕

**To make *Framed Alphabet*,
see page 88.**

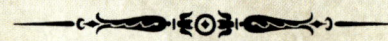

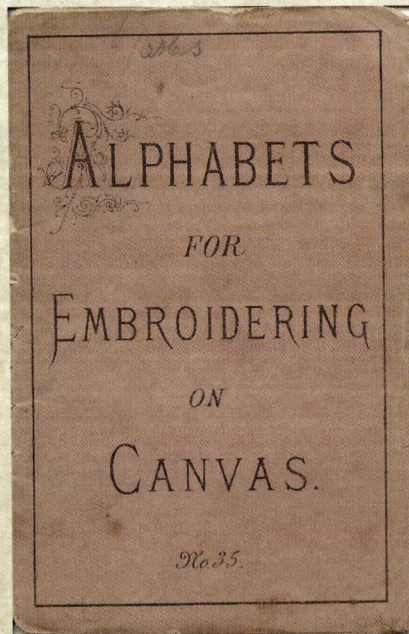

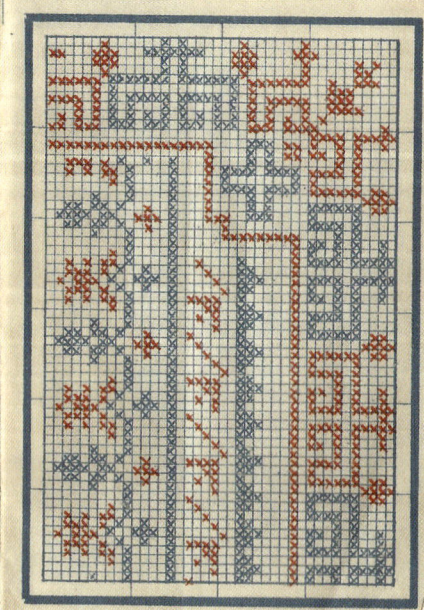

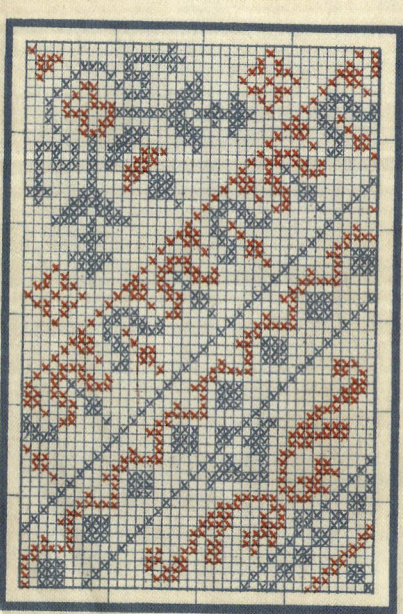

FOR MY FRIEND BY FELICIANA

For My Friend is the first sampler Feliciana stitched for Emily. Before sending the sampler to her friend in Tucson, Feliciana sent small, colored images she had created on grid paper showing the various motifs she planned to use.

To read Chapter 1,
see page 12.

■ FINISHED SIZE

8½" × 5¾"

■ STITCH COUNT

139W × 90H

■ SUPPLIES

13" × 10" — 36ct. Stitches and Spice Camofudge

■ SYMBOLS

Crescent Colours Belle Soie		DMC approximations
▾	Mahogany	3045
●	Cranberry	3685
⊤	Mudpie	3046
♣	Creme de Menthe	3345 & 3346
⌄	Fern Frond	503
⊍	Maple Leaf	356
○	Angel Blush	950
┃	Baguette	746
◥	Noir	535
⚘	Her Crowne	833

Designed by unknown girl, likely mid-19th century

Reproduced and stitched by Linda Danielson

◼ INSTRUCTIONS

Center the design on the linen. Cross stitch with
1 strand of cotton or silk over 2 threads of linen except
for the flower bouquet top right. This is stitched over
1 thread of linen.

When finished, the sampler can be hem stitched on all
sides or framed. See page 90 for finishing instructions.

○ BS Angel Blush   ⚘ BS Her Crowne

ı BS Baguette   ▾ BS Mahogany

● BS Cranberry   ∪ BS Maple Leaf

♣ BS Creme de Menthe   ⊤ BS Mudpie

∨ BS Fern Frond   ◄ BS Noir

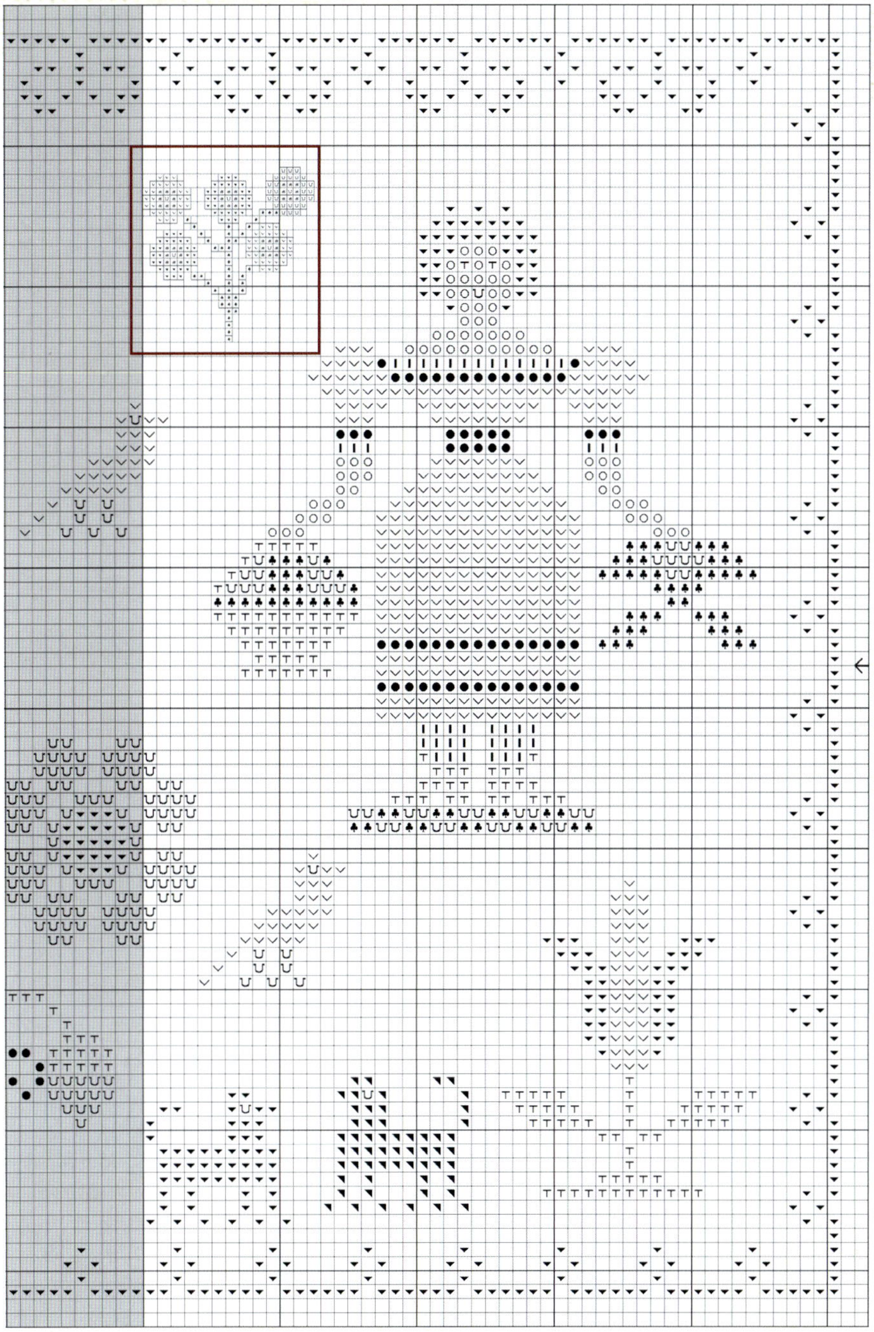

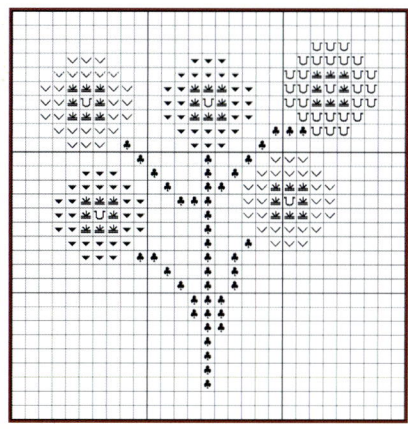

Detailed flower chart

*Gray bar
represents repeat*

FOR MY FRIEND BY EMILY

After Feliciana sent Emily a small hem-stitched silk-on-linen sampler and sketches based on that project, Emily reworked some of the elements and created a sampler with her friend prominently placed as the center motif.

To read Chapter 2, see page 16.

▦ FINISHED SIZE

7" × 4½"

▦ STITCH COUNT

139W × 90H

▦ SUPPLIES

11" × 8" — 20ct. Weeks Dye Works Straw

▦ SYMBOLS

The Gentle Art (overdyed cotton)	DMC approximations
★ Acorn 1111	938
♥ Weathered Barn 7046	3685
◣ Pine 0120	501
ʙ Baby Spinach 7050	3363
ɜ Fragrant Cloves 7026	920
ʍ Woodrose 7018	3064
= Chamomile 7016	642
■ Onyx 7063	3799
◄ Brethren Blue 7004	930
· GA Oatmeal 1140	3866

Designed by Linda Danielson and Vickie LoPiccolo Jennett

Stitched by Vickie LoPiccolo Jennett

▨ INSTRUCTIONS

Center the design on the linen. Cross stitch with
1 strand of cotton over 1 thread of linen.

When finished, the sampler can be hem stitched on all
sides or framed. See page 90 for finishing instructions.

★ GA Acorn

ᴮ GA Baby Spinach

♥ GA Brethren Blue

= GA Chamomile

♥ GA Weathered Barn

³ GA Fragrant Cloves

· GA Oatmeal

■ GA Onyx

◣ GA Pine

ᴎ GA Woodrose

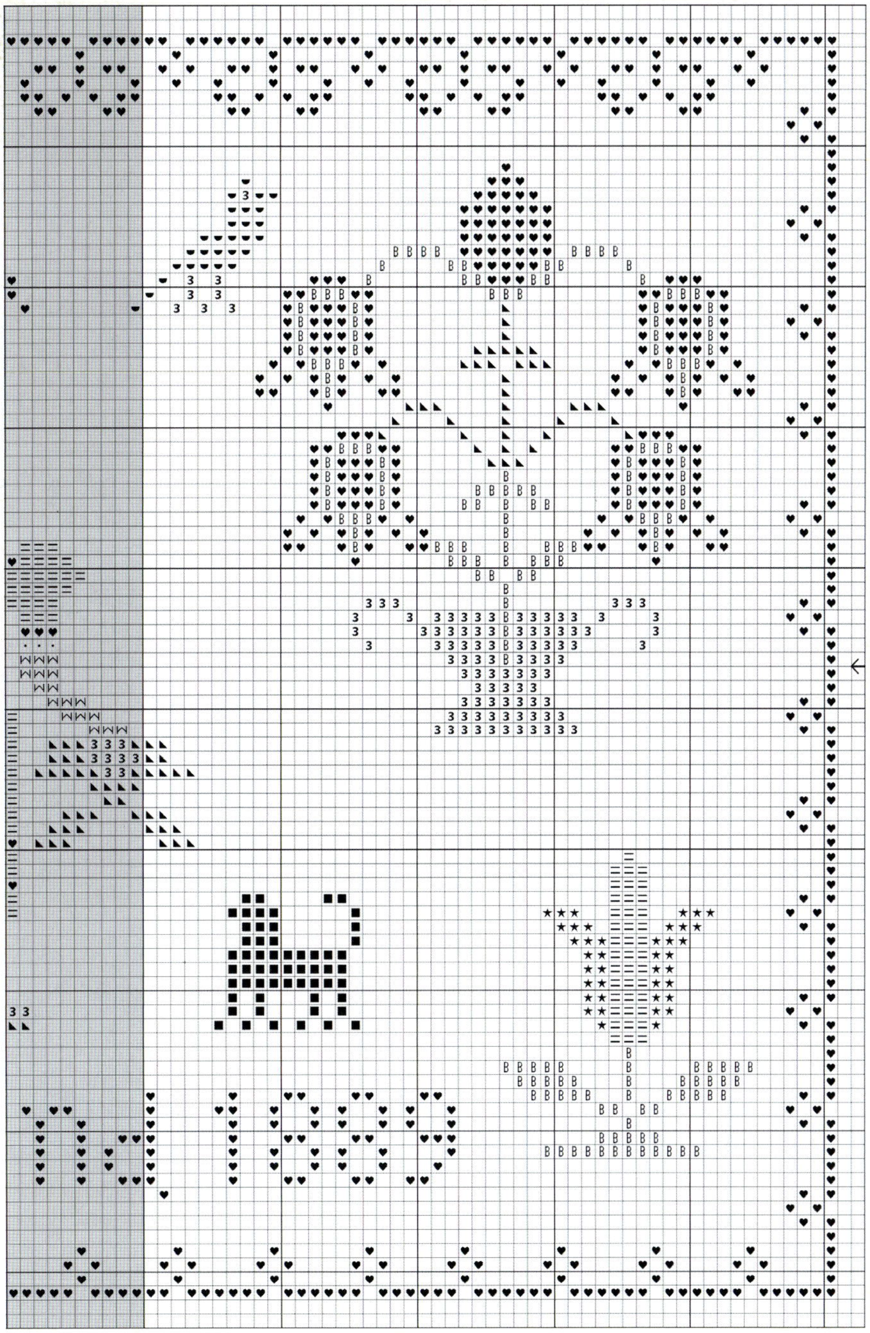

Gray bar
represents repeat

SONORAN BORDERS SAMPLER

The motifs in this sampler represent the Sonoran desert ranch where Feliciana spent the early years of her life. Not having any photographs, she relied on a small sampler made by an aunt to represent the sheltering trees, a beloved dog, flowers, a water pump and a house, among other motifs. Although the actual provenance is unknown, the antique upon which this project is based is believed to be from Mexico.

To read Chapter 3, see page 19.

FINISHED SIZE

8¾" × 5"

STITCH COUNT

175W × 99H

SUPPLIES

13" × 9" — 40ct. Lakeside Linens Vintage Sand Dune

SYMBOLS

The Gentle Art (overdyed cotton)	DMC approximations
⁄ Shaker White 7025	3866
⌂ Brandy 0540	729
- Apple Cider 7041	167
• Endive 7080	730
ₚ Pecan Pie 7097	610
↓ Portabella 7076	3790
✗ Pomegranate 7019	3721 (dark) and 223 (light)

Adapted from the 1876 sampler by
Maria Rificacao Pacheco

Stitched by Maegan Jennett

▪ INSTRUCTIONS

Center the design on the linen. Cross stitch with
1 strand of cotton over 2 threads of linen.

When finished, the sampler can be hem stitched on all
sides or framed. See page 90 for finishing instructions.

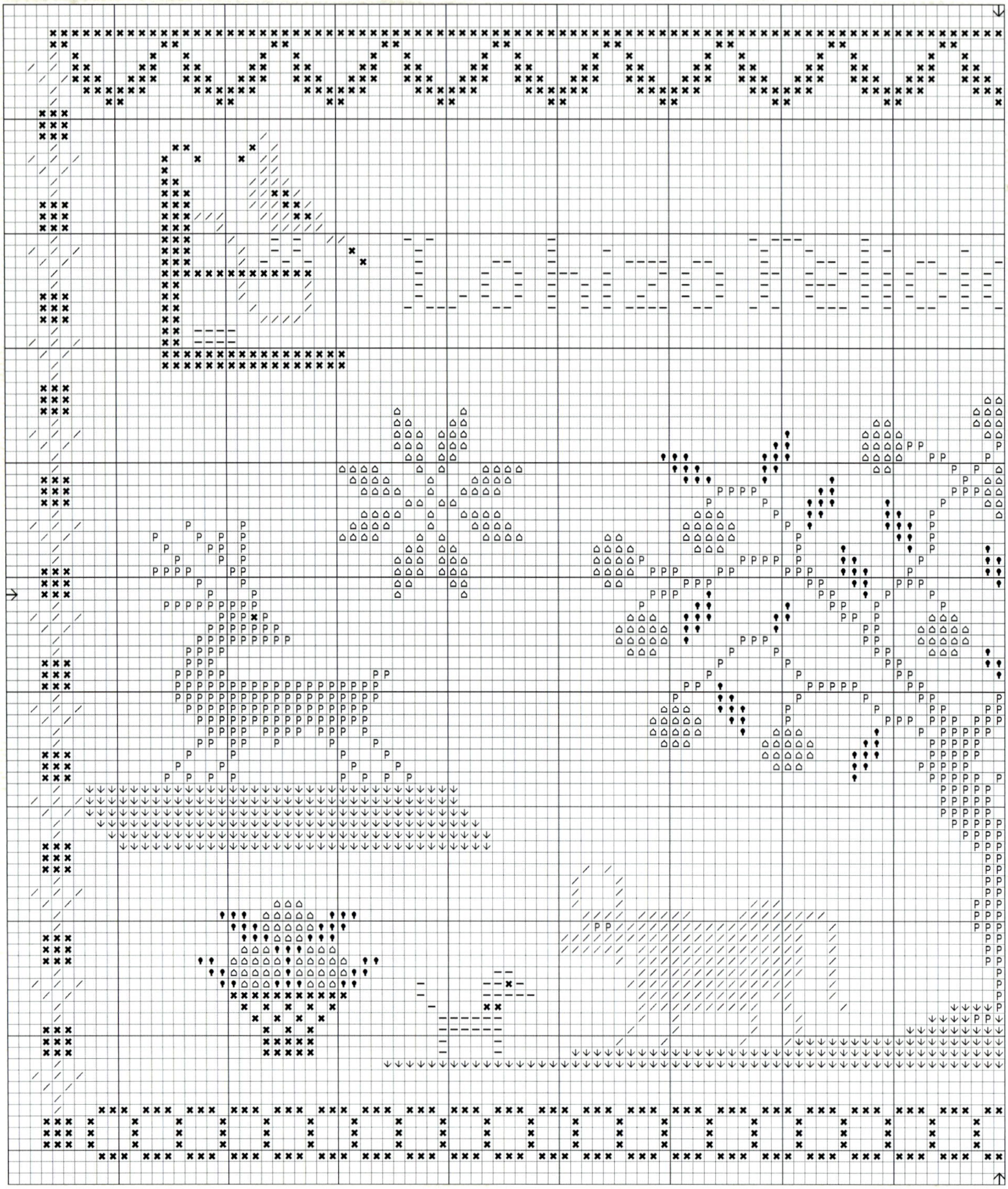

- GA Apple Cider   • GA Endive   ✗ GA Pomegranate

⌂ GA Brandy   ᵖ GA Pecan Pie   ↓ GA Portabella

∕ GA Shaker White

Gray bar
represents repeat

VELVET SCRAP EMERY AND PINCUSHION

To read Chapter 4,
see page 22.

Both Emily and Feliciana took pleasure in creating useful items from bits and pieces of fabric, ribbon and thread. Actual antique velvet sewing accessories inspired these projects. The original emery is decorated with a painted floral wreath and topped with layers of delicate silk ribbon. The pincushion is decorated with perle cotton tied and gathered in the center with a twisted design.

◼ PINCUSHION SIZE

5" × 4½" × 1¾"

◼ EMERY SIZE

2" × 4"

◼ SUPPLIES FOR TWO PROJECTS

2 scraps of velvet: 1 approximately 8" square and 1 approximately 6" square.

1 — 6" square of coordinating sturdy fabric

1 skein of coordinating 6-strand cotton or DMC #5 perle cotton color 221

20" coordinating trim, braid or cording*

60" — ½" wide lightweight coordinating ribbon

2 cups emery "sand" or finely ground walnut shells

40 or 50 wt all purpose cotton, rayon or polyester coordinating sewing thread

Sewing needle

Rug needle

The braid can be made with your favorite cording tool — a lucet or cording drill — using DMC #5 perle cotton in a single or multiple colors.

◼ ELONGATED STRAWBERRY EMERY

The shape of this strawberry is based on an antique velvet emery with a hand-painted flower wreath around the center. Once you see the ease of constructing a strawberry, you'll want to make them to accompany a variety of projects. Size is easy to adjust — cut a smaller fabric square for a smaller strawberry and a larger square if you want a larger strawberry.

Cut an 8" circle from the 8" square of velvet. Fold in half. Cut the circle in half across the middle fold. You will have enough fabric to make two strawberries.

Fold one of the semicircles in half, right sides together. Machine or hand sew together the 2 straight edges of the velvet. If hand sewing, use small, close stitches.

Designed by Vickie Jennett
Finished by Kathy Norton

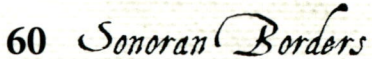

Flip inside out and sew a running stitch across the open edge of the velvet. You will use the extra thread, so do not cut or tie off. Once the running stitch is complete, gently pull the thread to gather the fabric. Leave enough space to pour emery or ground walnut stuffing into the strawberry.

Hint: A small funnel is a great way to pour the contents into the strawberry.

When full, pull the thread taut along the stitching so the velvet gathers around the stuffing. Tack down the gathers to make the top as smooth as possible. Close the top of the strawberry.

In a traditional strawberry, a star-shaped piece of felt typically is applied to the top to resemble leaves. This strawberry, like the antique, is topped with ribbon. For a flat look like the antique, sew layers of ribbon around the top of the strawberry, beginning about ¾" down and tacking around in layers until covering the top. Tie a bow and tack down with a few anchor stitches.

For a gathered look like the new strawberry, sew a running stitch along the top edge of 60" length of ribbon, gathering lightly as you go. Then tack the ribbon to the top of the strawberry in the same method as above.

RECTANGULAR EMERY PIN CUSHION

Trim the 6" velvet and the coordinating fabric to 6" × 5½" and place right sides together. Using a ½" seam allowance, sew around the rectangles leaving a 1" opening at the corner. Turn it right-side out.

Use the eraser end of pencil, if needed, to push out the corners. Fill with emery powder or ground walnut shells. Blind stitch the opening shut.

Tack the braid or cording trim around all sides of pincushion. Wrap perle cotton around the rectangle as if wrapping a package. Pull tight and anchor by taking several stitches up and down through the center of the pincushion (use heavy tapestry needle or rug needle), pulling tight to create a tuck. To finish the center, wrap several inches of braided or corded perle cotton in a circle and tack to pincushion using coordinating sewing thread.

FROM MY LOVING HANDS

To read Chapter 5,
see page 26.

Hands were a prominent image in Victorian culture. Certainly daily chores and labor required extensive use of hands. But hands often were romanticized and pictured holding bouquets or reaching out in friendship to another. This blackwork piece truly represents hands reaching out across the miles in an expression of friendship between Feliciana and Emily.

■ SIZE

3½" × 2⅜"

■ STITCH COUNT

29W × 34H

■ SUPPLIES

1 rectangular Tokens and Trifles 20ct. perforated paper sewing card

See page 90 for backstitch instructions.

■ SYMBOLS

The Gentle Art (overdyed cotton)	DMC approximations
– Pine 0120	501
– Buckeye Scarlet 0390	304
– Gold Leaf 0420	783
– Onyx 7063	939
– Blue Jay 0210	826

Designed and stitched by Vickie LoPiccolo Jennett

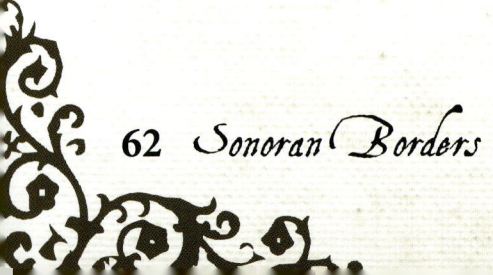

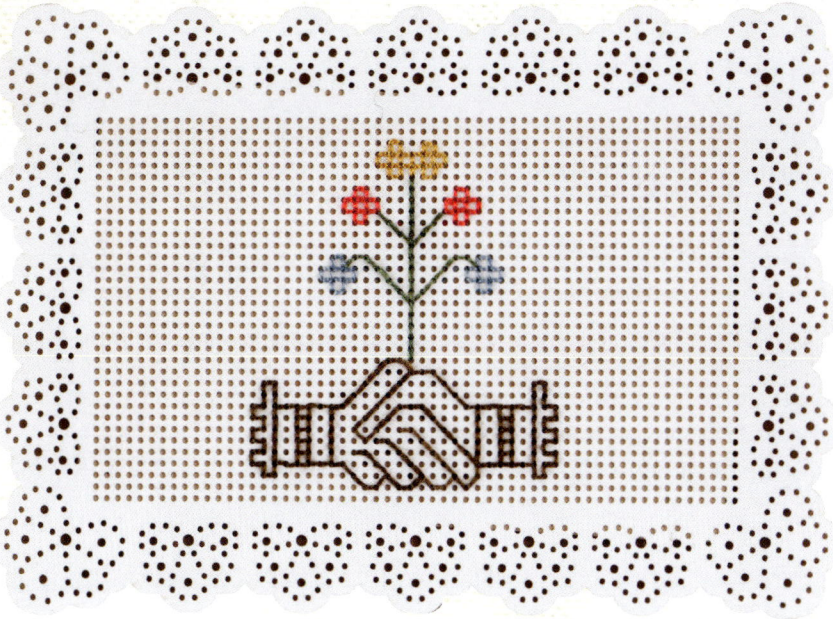

◼ INSTRUCTIONS

Center the design on the card. Back stitch the design. Attach the card to paper or fabric backing if desired.

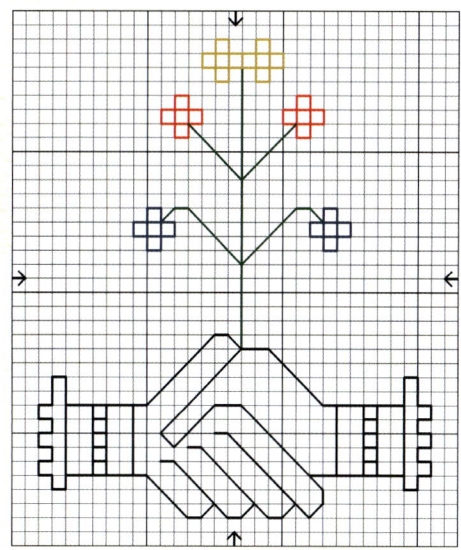

– GA Buckeye Scarlet

– GA Blue Jay

– GA Gold Leaf

– GA Pine

– GA Onyx

PEACOCK PINCUSHION

As Feliciana walked through the streets and gardens of San Francisco, she longed to be able to share the fragrant and colorful flowers she saw with Emily. Although she dried and pressed a few, she also stitched a tiny pin cushion with free-form flowers for her friend. In return, Emily created a small but whimsically colored peacock, reminiscent of the ones Feliciana talked about, as well as the ones she occasionally saw in Tucson. She used scraps of a handkerchief that had been her father's to complete the pincushion.

Throughout history, the peacock had been a symbol of immortality, renewal, protection and enlightenment. Some also associate the peacock with purity, pride and vanity. For centuries and across cultures, it has appeared in tapestry, needlework and samplers. Only two colors are used to stitch this stylized peacock. An old silk handkerchief was used for the back of the pincushion and two coordinating sides. Scraps of blue silk fabric were used for the two other sides. Both silk and cotton floss options are provided below.

**To read Chapter 6,
see page 30.**

SIZE

3½" × 3½"

STITCH COUNT

31W × 29H

SUPPLIES

4 — 1½" × 4" strips of coordinating fabric

1 — 4½" × 4½" piece of blue fabric for backing

4 — 4" pieces of coordinating silk ribbon, approximately ¼" wide

About 1 cup fiberfill (or desired soft filling for pin cushion)

Sewing thread for finishing

4" × 4" square — 40ct. Lakeside Linens Vintage Luna

SYMBOLS

Silk	DMC approximations
· Gloriana Pacific Blue Dark #173	312
· Gloriana Crimson #149	347

Stitched by Unknown Needleworker, likely 19th century

Designed by Vickie LoPiccolo Jennett

Finished by Kathy Norton

■ INSTRUCTIONS

Center the design on the linen. Cross stitch using 1 strand of silk or cotton over 2 strands of linen.

The stitched peacock will become the center front of the pincushion. Trim to 2½" square.

Lay the peacock square face up. Place a coordinating strip right-side down, on right side of peacock piece. Line up top edges. Using a ¼" seam allowance, start sewing at the dot and continue to the bottom. Press to the strip.

Align the second coordinating strip right-side down on the bottom of the unit. Sew together across the bottom. Press to the strip.

Continue with the left and top side strips in the same manner. When you get back to the first strip, finish sewing the seam to create the pincushion top. Trim to 4½" square.

Place the backing fabric right-side down on the pieced top of the pincushion, aligning the edges. Stitch around the outside edge of the pincushion using ¼" seam allowance. Keep a 2" opening on one side for turning.

Turn the project to the right sides and ease corners.

Stuff the cushion with batting material of your choice. Hand stitch the opening closed.

Sew pieces of ribbon to each corner. With embroidery thread, place a stitch through the center of the cushion several times and finish on the top side with a French knot.

Finish

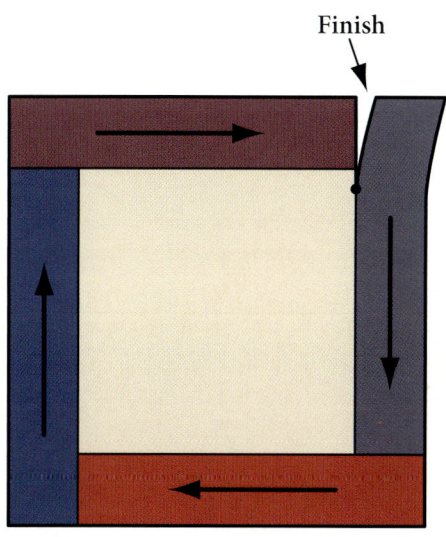

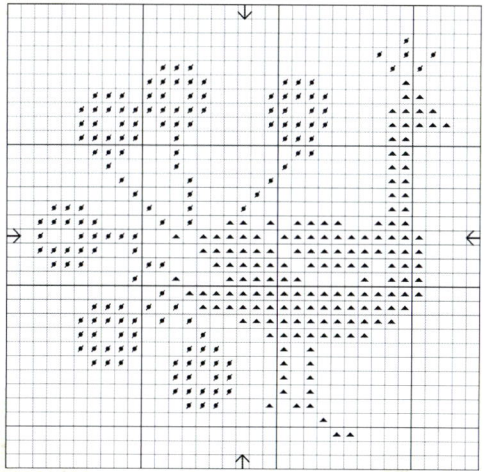

- Gloriana Crimson 149
- Gloriana Pacific Blue Dark 173

DEER TO MY HEARTS TABLE MAT

Family, friends and food formed the foundation of Emily and Feliciana's lives. After learning sewing techniques in school, Feliciana decided to make a table mat to send to Emily. The simple design was created to be a functional table mat to place under hot dishes so they would not mar the table. The small motifs are taken both from her aunt's antique sampler, as well as a beaded spot motif sampler that included a deer with a flower in its mouth.

Interestingly enough, fashioning a square piece of linen into a diamond-shaped space is simple but not necessarily intuitive. Somehow those of us who are accustomed to making crosses in a box want to turn the linen on an angle to make everything turn out all right. This just doesn't work. What does work, though, is stitching these simple motifs and using a square template turned on its side to cut. The motifs on this little table mat are taken from two of the antique pieces featured in this book.

To read Chapter 7, see page 34.

■ SIZE

16" × 9½"

■ STITCH COUNT

15W × 22H

■ SUPPLIES

6 fat quarters (or scraps) of different printed cotton fabric (2 dark, 2 medium, 2 light; reserve one 19" × 11" piece for backing)

Sewing thread for finishing

2 — 5" × 5" squares, 30ct. Weeks Dye Works Cocoa Linen

■ SYMBOLS

The Gentle Art (overdyed cotton)	DMC approximations
• Garden Gate 7067	3781
• Buckeye Scarlet 0390	304
▴ Pine 0120	501

Designed and stitched by Vickie LoPiccolo Jennett
Finished by Kathy Norton

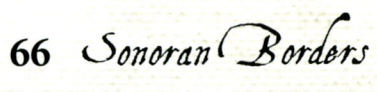

![quilted cross-stitch table runner with holiday motifs]

■ INSTRUCTIONS

Cross stitch each design on a piece of 5" square linen with 1 strand of cotton over 2 threads of linen. Trim each motif to 2¾" square making sure the motif is on point.

From the fat quarters or scraps, cut 21 total — 2¾" squares (allows for ¼" seams).
8 — assorted darks
7 — assorted lights
6 — assorted mediums

Referring to the diagram on page 68, lay out each 2¾" × 2¾" square in the order they will be sewn. Sew into diagonal rows. Join the rows pressing to one side.

Lay the backing fabric and pieced front right sides together. On the pieced side, sew with a ¼" seam allowance around the project. Leave an opening at the end of row 1 for turning. Trim away the excess backing fabric to match the pieced front and clip all points. Be careful to clip the inside points only to the stitching and remove any excess fabric to help the project lay flat.

Turn the project carefully through the opening at the end of row #1. Ease the points in place and press. Fold the ends at turning point in and pin in place. Press.

Top stitch around the outside of the project ⅛" to ¼" from the outer edge.

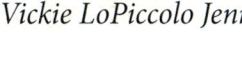

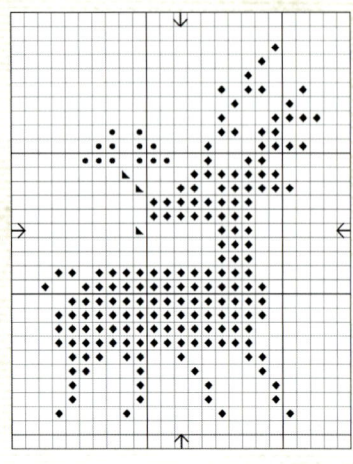

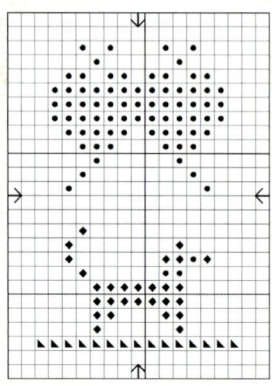

- GA Buckeye Scarlet
- GA Garden Gate
- GA Pine

Hearts
& Dog

Deer

Mention the territories. *Washington, Idaho, Montana, Dakota, Indian, New Mexico, Arizona, Utah, Wyoming, and Colorado.*
Bound Washington. What is its capital? How is Olympia situated?
Bound Idaho. What is its capital? How is Boise City situated?
Bound Montana. What is its capital? How is Virginia situated?
Bound Dakota. What is its capital? How is Yankton situated?
Bound Indian Territory. Wh⸺ ⸺ ⸺ ⸺it from Texas?
Bound New Mexico. ⸺ ⸺ ⸺anta Fe situated?
Bound Arizona. ⸺ ⸺ated?
Bound Utah. ⸺ ⸺ated?
Bound Wy⸺ ⸺ated?

SIMPLE SEWING ROLLUP

Often called a huswif, or housewife, the original may date as far back as the Civil War era. Women, girls and sometimes even men carried huswifs as a place to store buttons and other small sewing supplies. Two versions are provided here — the one Feliciana made as a project in school and one she made at home for Emily, which included linen pockets that were cross stitched with border designs from an antique Mexican or Spanish sampler.

The instructions below are provided for the stitched rollup. To make the fabric version, simply substitute two pieces of printed fabric for the linen pockets.

To read Chapter 8,
see page 38.

■ SIZE

4" × 15"

■ STITCH COUNT

Vine — 44W × 23H
Flower with year — 37W × 22H

■ SUPPLIES

2 — 7" × 8" pieces 28ct. Cashel Sandcastle linen

6 different coordinating printed fabrics:

    1 strip of fabric at least 1" × 36" bias strip for binding

    1 — 3½" × 15½" print for outside

    1 — 3½" × 4" print for center pocket
    (3 if not inserting linen pockets)

    2 — 3½" × 4" pieces of the same print
    (1 for the bottom pocket and 1 for the top lining)

20" ribbon for tie

■ SYMBOLS

The Gentle Art (overdyed cotton)	DMC approximations
◆ Garden Gate 7067	3781
◆ Blackboard 7051	939
◣ Pine 0120	501
◻ Weathered Barn 7046	3685

*Reproduced from an antique
by Vickie LoPiccolo Jennett*

Stitched by Andrea Uustalu

INSTRUCTIONS

Center each design on one piece of linen. Cross stitch with 1 strand of cotton over 2 threads of linen. Trim to 3½" × 4".

Use the template found on page 73 to cut the top curve of 15½" outside print and top inside lining piece. Make ¼" double-fold hem at the bottom of the inside lining piece.

Make a ¼" double-fold hem at the top and bottom of each of the four pockets, including the linen ones. Hand or machine hem both the top and bottom.

Starting at the top (curve), place the inside lining piece and backing fabric wrong-sides together. Arrange each pocket to overlap the next (alternate printed fabric with linen if selecting this option), so that approximately 3" of each shows. If desired, baste together sides. Sew down bottom of each pocket.

Cut a 1"-wide bias strip at least 36" long and make ½"-wide single fold bias tape. Bind the rollup with the single fold bias tape.

Fold the ribbon tie in half. Tack to center top curved end of the rollup.

PROJECT 8

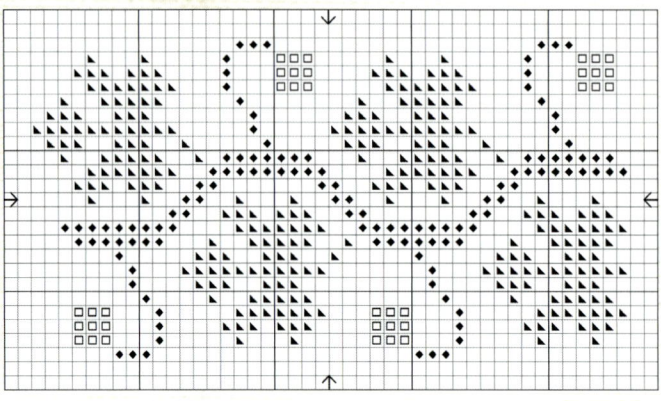

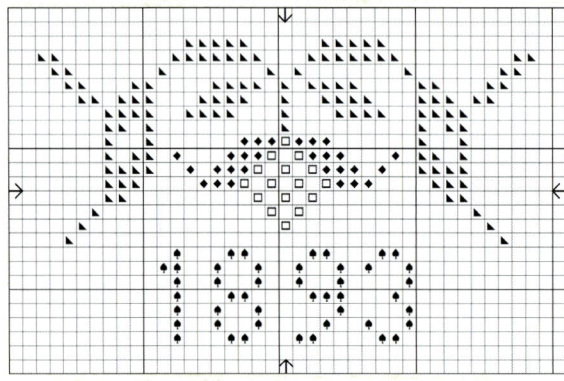

- GA Blackboard
- GA Garden Gate
- GA Pine
- GA Weathered Barn

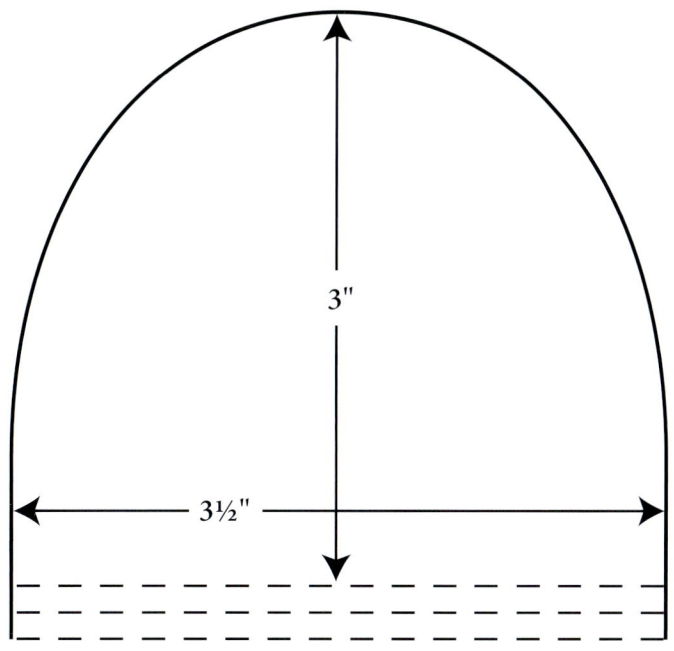

3"

3½"

Hem allowance
Turn under and
hem to create
piece 3" high.

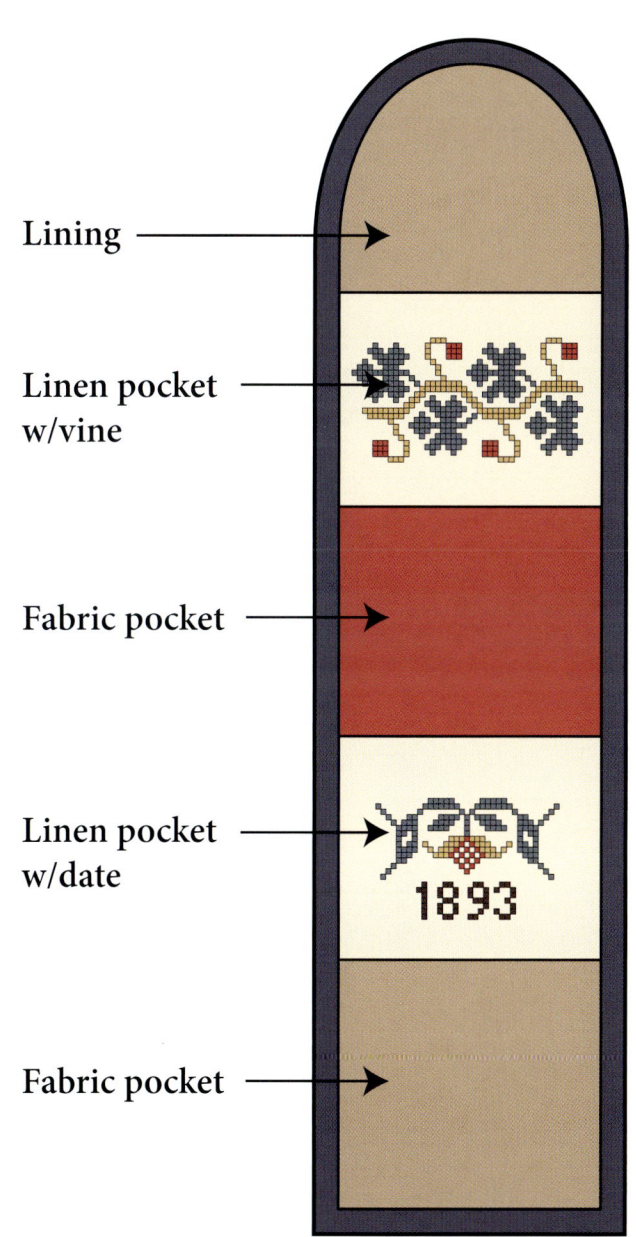

Lining

Linen pocket
w/vine

Fabric pocket

Linen pocket
w/date

1893

Fabric pocket

LAS PALOMAS BLANCAS PURSE

This small and useful purse was a gift from Emily to commemorate Feliciana's marriage to Hector. It combines motifs from samplers the girls made for one another shortly after they met. (When constructing the purse, referring to the color photographs of both sides is helpful.)

To read Chapter 9, see page 41.

■ SIZE

7¾" × 13½"

■ STITCH COUNT

85W × 164H

■ SUPPLIES

3 — 8" × 12" pieces 32ct. Lakeside Linens Vintage Examplar

½ yard cotton print fabric for lining and binding

2 fat quarters coordinating print fabric

1 — 7" length cord elastic

3 small shank buttons

1 — 10" × 15" piece lightweight iron-on facing

1 — 5" × 5" piece wool or linen for needle-pages

■ SYMBOLS

The Gentle Art (overdyed cotton)	DMC approximations
♣ Tomato 058	919
✖ Forest Glade 0190	936
◂ Dried Thyme 0110	470
ᴘ Pecan Pie 7097	610
· Oatmeal 1140	712
ᴎ Wood Smoke 1130	841
ʟ Gold Leaf 0420	783

✺✳✦✳✦✳✦✳✦✳✦✳✦✺✦✳

Designed by Vickie LoPiccolo Jennett

Stitched by Sandy Bortz

Assembled by Kathy Norton

■ INSTRUCTIONS

Center each design on 1 piece of linen. Cross stitch with 2 strands of cotton over 2 threads of linen. (Each linen section of the purse was stitched individually and pieced to create a definitive fold.)

Cut each stitched piece to 5" × 12", making certain each design is centered. Arrange the stitched pieces as shown in the diagram on page 80, making sure placement is correct. Sew together with ¼" seam allowance to create the outside of the purse. Press seams open from wrong side. Using the purse template, cut a piece of iron-on interfacing. Center on the wrong side of the stitched piece, aligning the straight edge of the interfacing with the straight end (lettering). Follow the manufacturer's instructions and fuse the interfacing to the wrong side of stitched piece. Trim stitched piece to size of interfacing.

Using the purse template, cut the lining fabric. Place lining on the stitched piece (outside of purse), wrong sides together, and baste ⅛" from all edges.

For the bottom pocket with the flap, use the shortened purse template to cut 2 pieces of 1 of the coordinating fabrics. Starting at the top curved edge, place these 2 pieces wrong sides together and stitch with a ½" seam allowance around the top curved edge and ½" seam allowance along the bottom edge. Trim the seams along curved edge.

Turn the fabric right side out and press. Fold the bottom edge to the lower part of curved piece, forming an envelope with sides open. Baste the sides in place at the bottom or right side of lining piece. Leave the flap out of the seam.

For the center pocket, cut a 7" × 12" piece of the second coordinating fabric. Fold in half, wrong-sides together (3½" × 12") and press. Stitch ¼" from the top to form a casing for elastic. At the bottom, baste the edges together. Mark the center of fabric width. Fold 3 pleats into fabric so width of pocket will match width of stitched piece. Baste to hold the pleats in place.

Cut a 1½" × 7½" strip of the same fabric used for the pocket. Fold under ¼" along both long sides and press. Place the right-sides together and stitch long strip along bottom front of pocket. Turn remainder of strip to back side of pocket, encasing its bottom edge. Slip stitch in place.

Using a bodkin, thread the elastic through the top casing of pocket and secure at both ends.

Place the middle pocket on the lining piece, ¾" above the lower pocket. Baste along the sides to secure.

For the needlebook cover, use the template to cut 2 pieces of 1 coordinating fabric. Place fabric right sides together and stitch around outside edge using a ¼" seam allowance and leaving a 2" opening for turning. Trim seams at curve and turn right-side out. Blind stitch the opening closed. Fold in half and press.

For the needlebook pages, use the template to cut out one piece of wool or linen with pinking shears. Blanket stitch around edges if needed. Fold piece almost in half, so top piece is shorter than the back piece. Press.

Place the pages inside the needlebook cover, matching up folds. Stitch along fold line. Place the needlebook on top of the lining piece, 1" above the middle pocket. Blind stitch along the folded edge of the needlebook to attach.

Cut a 2"-wide bias strip of lining fabric, at least 44" long. Press under ½" along each long side to make a 1"-wide bias tape. Place the bias tape and stitched piece right sides together, aligning the raw edges under the bias tape (where lettering is placed). Sew, using a ½" seam allowance and mitering bottom corners. Turn the bias tape to the inside and blind stitch folded edge to lining.

Use floss or perle cotton to make 3 thread-chain buttonhole loops. Apply to each flap and bottom of front curved section.

Sew on 1 button for each inside flap and 1 for the bottom front of purse.

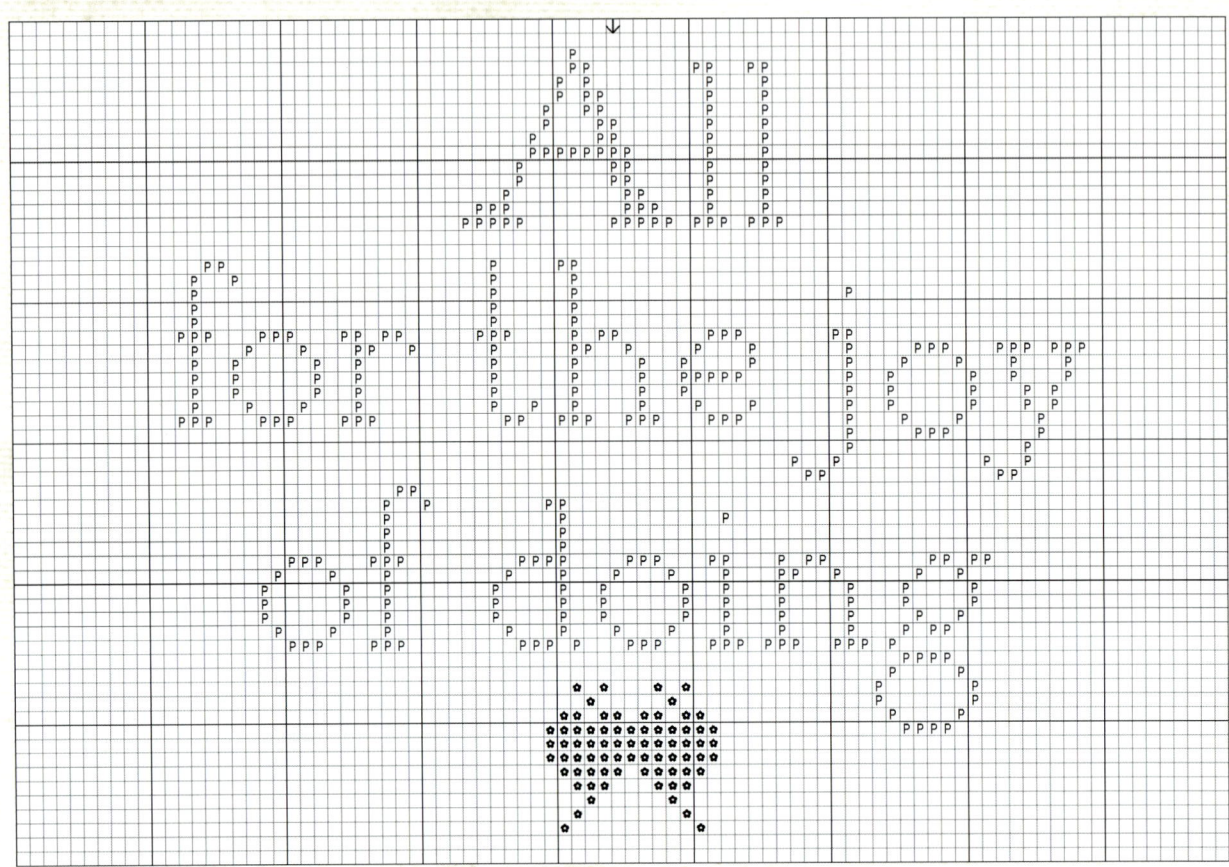

‹ GA Dried Thyme

✖ GA Forest Glade

∟ GA Gold Leaf

· GA Oatmeal

ᵖ GA Pecan Pie

✿ GA Tomato

⋈ GA Woodsmoke

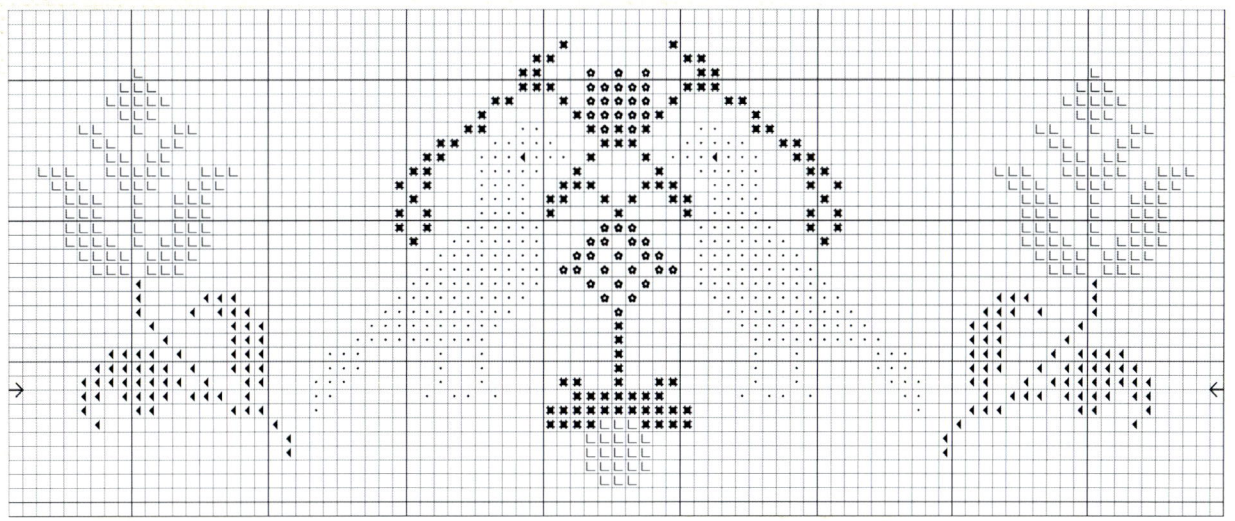

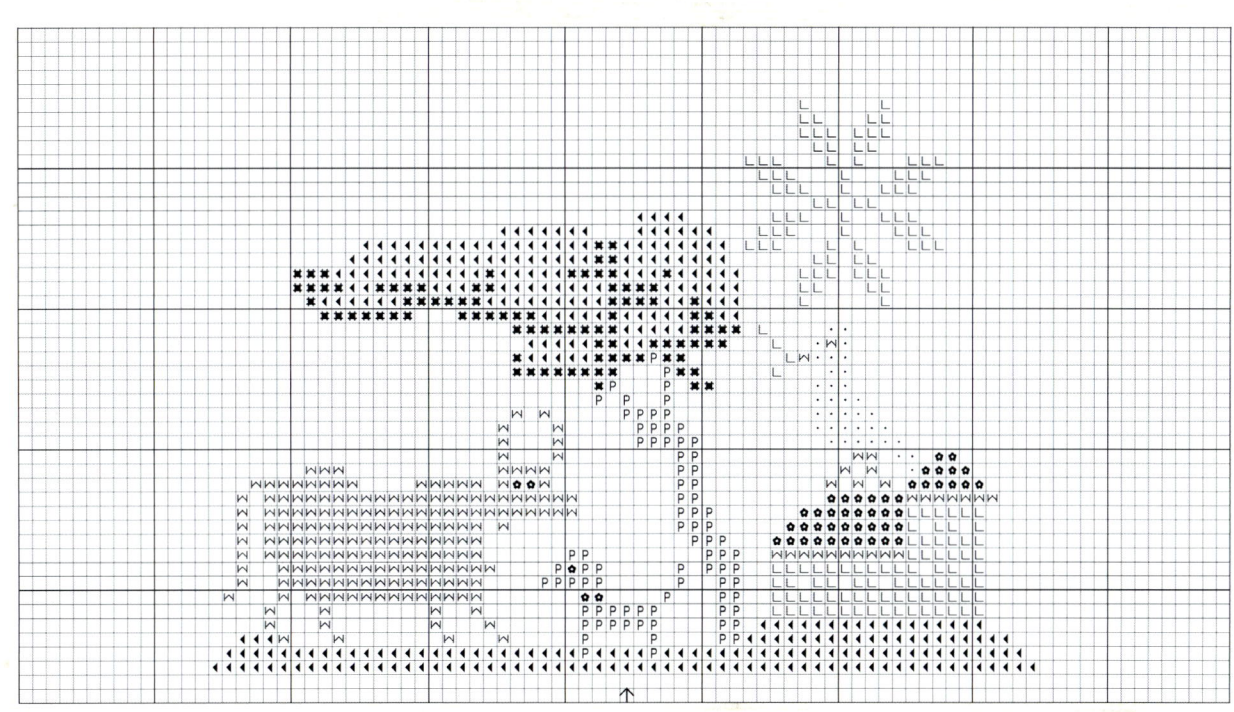

Outside Purse Placement Guide

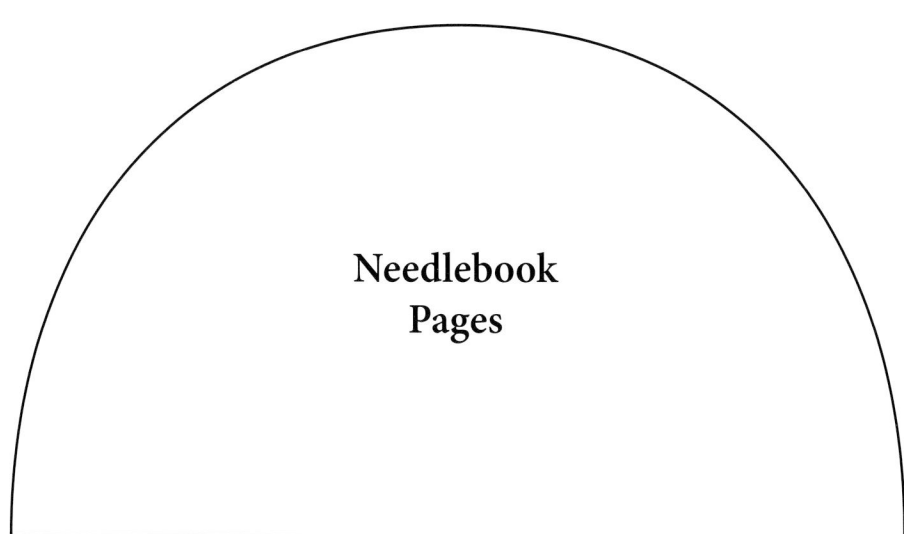

Needlebook
Pages

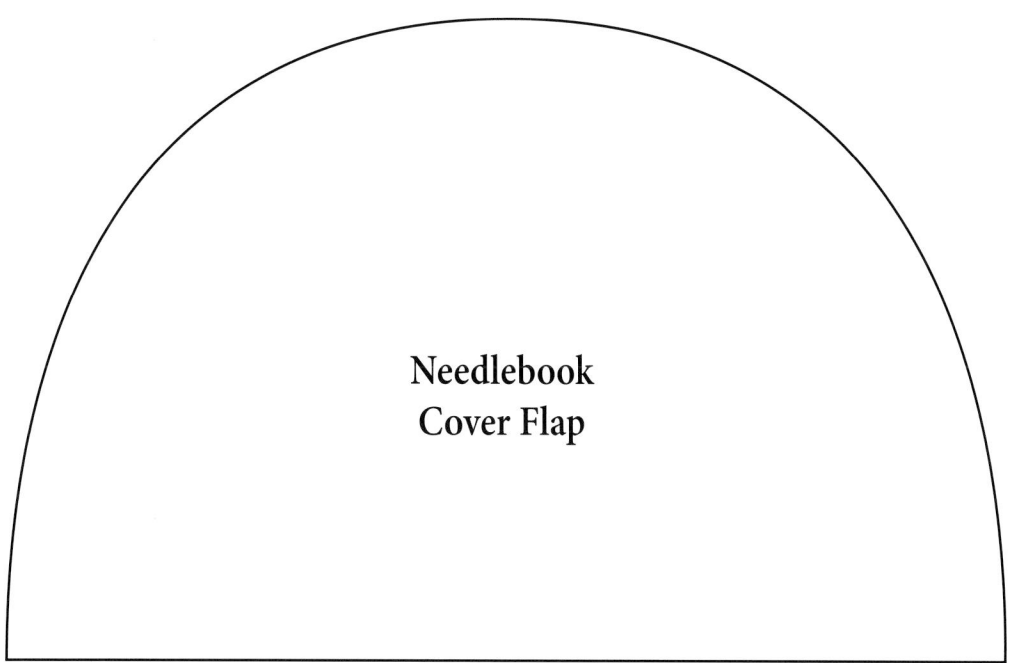

Needlebook
Cover Flap

Purse Needlebook Templates

Fold line

Purse Template

Join Purse template here

Inside Purse Template

Join Purse template here

Fold line

Cut along this line for bottom pocket only

Inside Purse Template

Perforated Paper Pieces

The stories of Emily's and Feliciana's lives were wrapped in the threads that formed small gifts sent through the mail during the early years of their friendship. Each of these items held personal meaning for the girls, and provided a creative and inexpensive way to let the other know how special she was.

Each of these projects was inspired by an antique stitched with various media on different backgrounds. The original bird was stitched in wool as part of a Victorian perforated paper spot motif sampler — the same size and color paper as that used in the projects. The stag was originally a bright purple beaded deer intricately worked on a cotton ground in a Mexican spot motif sampler. The flower pot was haphazardly but charmingly stitched over multiple threads of linen and fashioned into a diamond-shaped pin keep. The *Forget Me Not* was a bookmark originally stitched for a loving aunt.

To read Chapter 10, see page 44.

Stitch Count

10a (Forget Me Not) — 52W × 25H
10b (Crow) — 21W × 26H
10c (Flower Pot) — 21W × 31H
10d (Deer) — 21W × 27H

Supplies

1 sheet 14ct. Natural Perforated Paper

Designed and stitched by Vickie LoPiccolo Jennett

Symbols

The Gentle Art (overdyed cotton)	DMC approximations
♠ Blackboard 7051	939
◑ Sable 1110	869
◣ Pine 0120	501
◆ Garden Gate 7067	3781
≤ Spring Grass 0180	368
• Buckeye Scarlet 0390	304
◑ Gold Leaf 0420	783
◀ Dried Thyme 0110 *(light sections)*	470
⋈ Midnight 0240	796

Symbols

Weeks Dye Works (overdyed cotton)	DMC approximations
⊂ Cornsilk 1123	822
✦ Monkey Grass 2168	3362
▽ Clockwork 2230	720
↘ Battleship 2108	414
Y Dutch Iris 23242 *(blue section)*	2342

INSTRUCTIONS

Cross stitch each design individually with 2 strands of cotton over 1 hole on the perforated paper.

Once stitched on paper, each of these designs may be framed, backed with fabric, wide ribbon or card stock, edged with trim or fastened to a card or box-top. *YES! PASTE* is an excellent choice for gluing the perforated paper project to wood, fabric or paper.

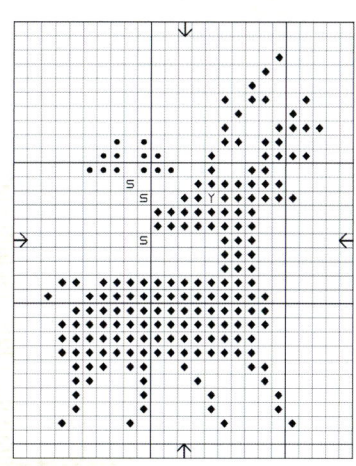

᾽ WDW Dutch Iris

♦ GA Garden Gate

ⱽ GA Spring Grass

• GA Buckeye Scarlet

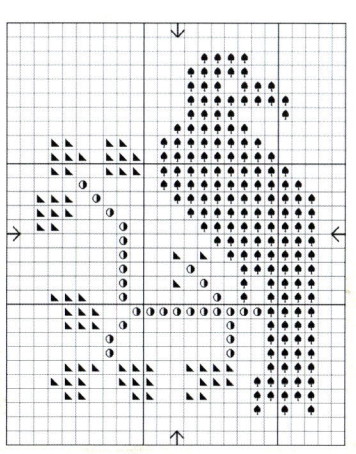

▸ GA Blackboard

◣ GA Pine

ₒ GA Sable

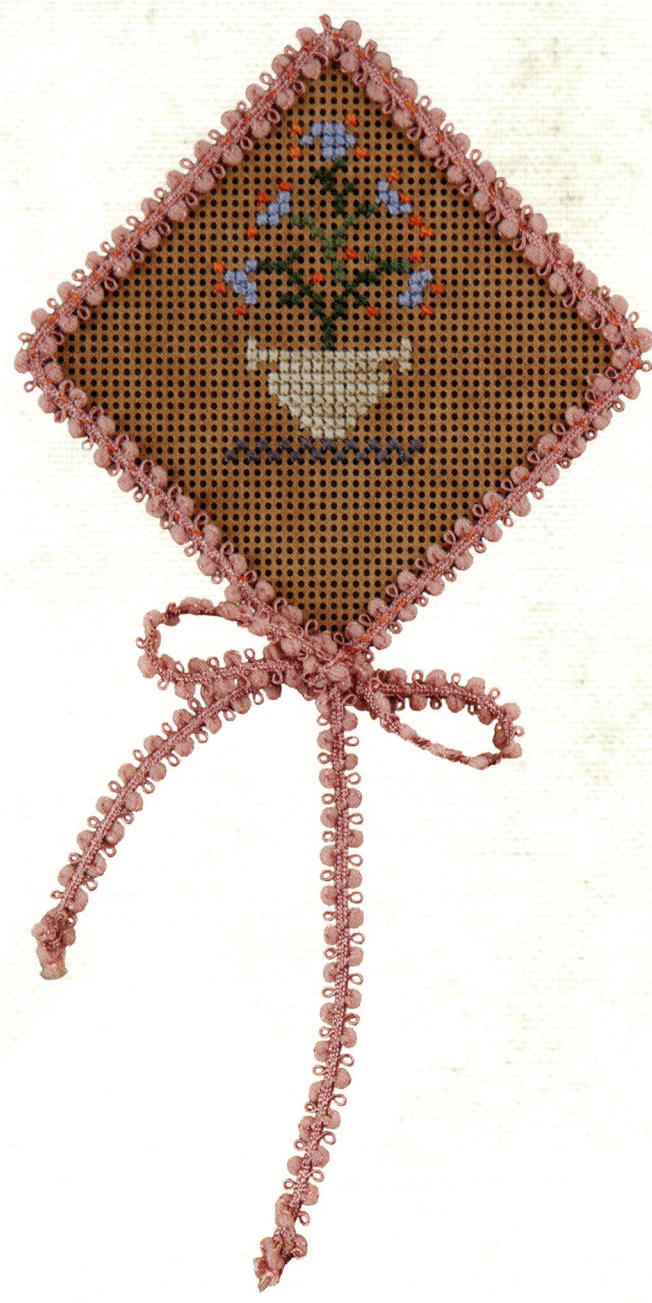

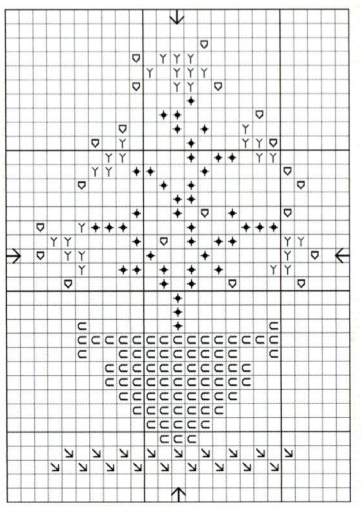

↘ WDW Battleship

◡ WDW Clockwork

⊂ WDW Cornsilk

⊼ WDW Dutch Iris

✦ WDW Monkey Grass

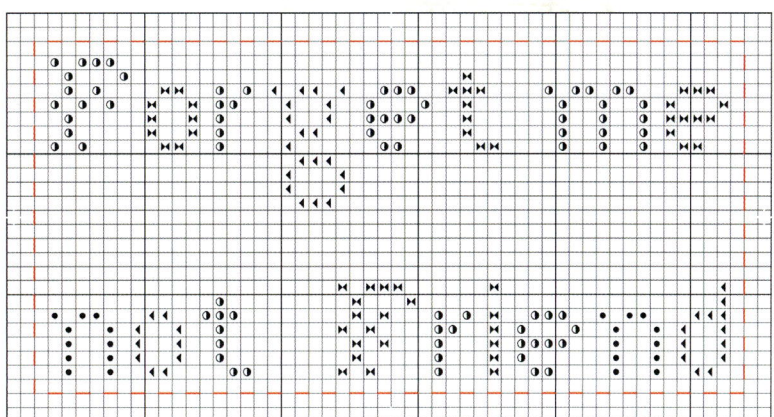

- GA Buckeye Scarlet
- GA Dried Thyme
- GA Midnight
- GA Gold Leaf

After stitching the words, trim the perforated paper with one row of holes along the outside. Attach the perforated paper to a piece of wide ribbon with a running stitch using two threads of Buckeye Scarlet.

FRAMED ALPHABET

In the story's epilogue, Feliciana's granddaughter, Anna, eventually makes a trip to the desert. Despite the passing years and ensuing events and milestones, she found the Sonoran desert much as her grandmother recalled. Likewise, the basic alphabet, so essential to those who stitch and write, remains a constant. Everyone can use an extra alphabet in their stitching bag, so these are provided for the times when an extra letter is needed to revise a name or a date.

To read the epilogue, see page 46.

SIZE

Each alphabet measures 4¼" × 3¼" when stitched on 14ct perforated paper

STITCH COUNT

Alphabet with upper case letters — 64W × 46H
Alphabet with lower case letters — 62W × 42H

SUPPLIES

1 sheet 14ct. ecru Perforated Paper

INSTRUCTIONS

Cross stitch with 2 strands of cotton or silk over 1 hole on the perforated paper. Frame to finish.

SYMBOLS

The Gentle Art (overdyed cotton)	DMC approximations
 * Blue Jay 0210	826

Designed and stitched by unknown 19th-century needleworker

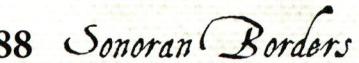

* GA Blue Jay

Helpful Hints

BACKSTITCH

The *From Loving Hands* project on page 62 uses a simple backstitch over one hole on perforated paper. The one difference between backstitch on paper and on fabric is that instead of sewing, each stitch is taken in an individual stabbing (up, down, up down) motion. This project is the perfect opportunity to try your hand at a very basic version of the blackwork technique. Although often worked as a double-running stitch, a simple over one back stitch over one hold on perforated paper is all that is needed. Make certain that all ends are neatly woven under stitches so they do not show from the front. (For further reference and a look at true Elizabethan blackwork, see **www.blackworkarchives.com**.)

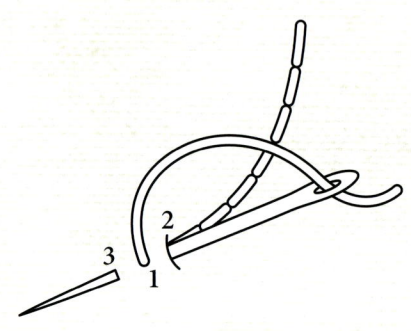

back stitch

BUTTONHOLE LOOP (also called *crocheted chain or thread loop*)

If you have never tried this technique, you may want to practice using a small crochet hook independent of your almost-finished *Las Palomas Blancas Purse* on page 74, then apply the finished loop. Create a loose slip knot with a 12" piece of floss. Wrap floss around head of the crochet hook and pull hook and floss through the front side of the slip knot. Pull the floss, wrap through slip knot and remove slipknot from hook, so only one wrap of floss remains. This forms the first link of the thread chain. Repeat the process, wrapping the floss around head of crochet hook, pulling the floss through previous chain, then slipping the previous chain off hook. Repeat until desired length is achieved. Fold the chain in half to form loop and attach to purse.

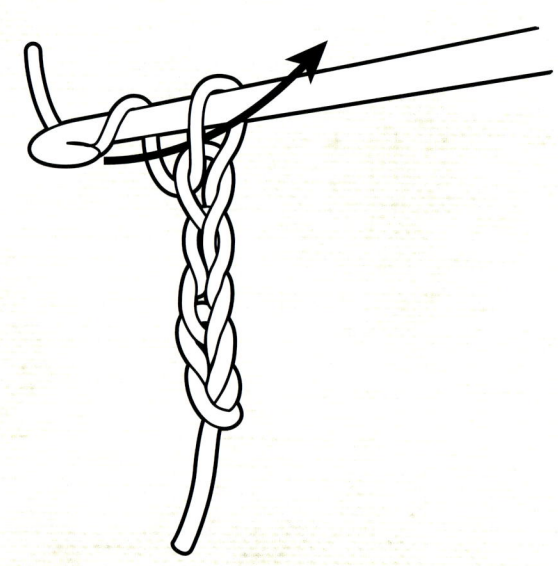

If you are experienced, see the color photo of the inside of the purse for placement and anchor the desired floss color at the center bottom of the purse and begin your crocheted chain stitch. This process is repeated for each inside flap of the purse.

CROSS STITCH

With the exception of the perforated paper projects and the top flower bouquet on *Feliciana's For My Friend* sampler on page 48, all cross stitch — punto de cruz — projects are executed over two threads of linen. Begin stitching on linen or paper in the most comfortable place for you. Some people begin in the center, others upper right, some lower left. You may prefer to complete a border before beginning on the inside motifs. What matters most is that each of your cross stitches is executed in the same direction (that is, all bottom stitches angling right and all top stitches angling left).

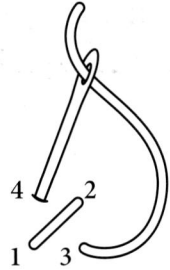

cross stitch

HEM STITCH

Many variations of the hem stitch exist. Likewise, extensive descriptions, on-line tutorials and classroom instruction detail execution of this method of finishing needlework. (One of the most helpful is published in *Linen Stitches* by the late and venerable Ginnie Thompson. Although out-of-print, the book frequently shows up on **www.amazon.com** or in used book stores.) Working a practice piece is a good idea before finishing a stitched project.

For the same width hemstitch used for *Feliciana's For My Friend* on page 48, measure 1" stitched border on all sides. Trim the excess linen. The following steps are completed on each side of the sampler: Begin on the top outside edge. Measure ¼" from the top. Start in the center of the row. Snip and pull a thread. (Use a needle to unweave if necessary.) Measure in another ¼". Cut and pull a thread. Repeat a third time so you will have three threads pulled. Repeat at bottom. Then on each side.

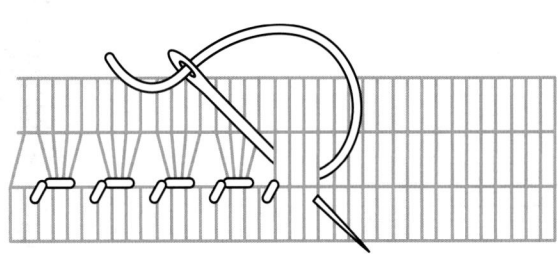

hem stitch

Fold under twice at the top, using the pulled thread row as fold lines. Press. The third pulled thread row (closest to stitching) becomes the channel for completing the hemstitch. Repeat folding and pressing on the bottom, then each side. Carefully trim bulk on corners if needed so they are smooth.

Using a thread that matches the linen, work the hemstitch on the wrong side of the linen. Bury knot in the folded linen. Working from left to right, pick up three linen threads and pull gently, catching the folded hem. Repeat this across the row. When arriving at the end, if fewer or more than three threads remain, take a compensating stitch picking up two threads. Turn the corner and continue around all four sides.

Sources and Supplies

For additional details or instruction regarding any of the techniques in *Sonoran Borders*, please visit your local needlework and/or quilting store — outstanding sources for classes and personal assistance. If you are unfamiliar with overdyed fibers, please note that color variations do exist.

The *Leisure Arts Embroidery Pocket Guide* is a basic illustrated guide to a variety of stitches.

Counted thread stores will be able to order 14ct *Mill Hill Perforated Paper* in ecru and antique brown, the two colors used in projects, as well as the *Tokens & Trifles* 20-ct perforated paper sewing cards.

Decorative ribbon for finishing perforated paper bookmarks is available through many sources. The ribbon used in the *Forget Me Not Friend* bookmark on page 84 is from Mokuba New York, 137 W. 38th St., New York, NY 10018.

If you are unfamiliar with creating and applying a binding, whether by hand or machine, instructions included with *The Whimsical Workshop Binding Tool* are useful. Available by calling (888) 499-5715.

On-line instructions provide information about making cording with a hook attached to a small drill. Threads also may be turned into cording with either a lucet or *The Spinster* (a tool designed specifically for this purpose). If not available locally, find *The Spinster* at **www.nordicneedle.com**. Check **www.priscillaspocket.com** for sources of their reproduction lucet.

Framing for projects in *Sonoran Borders* was completed by my local shop, Attic Needlework & Collectibles, 1837 W. Guadalupe Rd., Suite #109, Mesa, AZ 85202.

In addition to flea markets and antiques stores, vintage buttons can be found at local, state and national shows sponsored by The National Button Society or its chapters. For locations and dates, visit **www.nationalbuttonsociety.org**.

YES! PASTE is an acid-free glue that works well on paper and fabric. If you cannot find it in a craft store, visit **www.scrapbook.com**.

Reproduction milagros shown in photographs are by **www.pachamamasantafe.com**.

Bibliography

Research is formalized curiosity. It is poking and prying with a purpose.

—Zora Neale Hurston

Andrle, Patricia and Lesley Rudnicki. Sampler Motifs and Symbolism. Hillside Samplings, East Aurora, NY; 2003.

Beitz, Les. Treasury of Frontier Relics: A Collector's Guide. True Treasure Library, Conroe, TX; 1971

Bly, Nellie. Six Months in Mexico. Pittsburg Dispatch, Pittsburg, PA; 1888.

Egan, Martha. Milagros: Votive Offerings from the Americas. Museum of New Mexico Press, Santa Fe, NM; 1991.

Epple, Anne Orth. A Field Guide to the Plants of Arizona. The Globe Pwquot Press, Guilford, CT; 1995.

Goggin, Maureen Daley and Beth Fowkes Tobin, editors. Women and the Material Culture of Needlework and Textiles, 1750–1950. Ashgage Publishing Ltd., London, England; 2009.

Lauer, Charles D. Tales of Arizona Territory. Golden West Publishers, Phoenix, AZ; 1990.

Morgan, Anne Hodges and Rennard Strickland. Arizona Memories. The University of Arizona Press, Tucson, AZ; 1984.

Myres, Sandra L. Westering Women and the Frontier Experience 1800–1915. The University of New Mexico Press, Albuquerque, NM; 1999.

Olin, George. House in the Sun: A Natural History of the Sonoran Desert. Southwest Parks and Monument Association, Tucson, AZ; 1994.

Paré, Madeline Ferrin. Arizona Pageant: A Short History of the 48th State. Arizona Historical Foundation, Tempe, AZ; 1967.

Pinedo, Encarnacion and Strehl, Dan, editor. Encarnacion's Kitchen: Mexican Recipes from Nineteenth-Century California. University of California Press, Berkeley and Los Angeles, CA; 2003.

Serena, Raffaella. Embroideries and Patterns from 19th Century Vienna. Antique Collector's Club, Woodbridge, Suffolk, UK; 1988.

The Illustrated History of the 19th Century. Book Creation Illustrated Ltd., London, England; 2000.

Thompson, Ginnie. Linen Stitches. Gloria & Pat, Inc., 1987.

PHOTOS BY CHAD TURNER:
Back cover and pages 7, 11, 29, 69, 93 & 95.

About the Author

Vickie has been writing as long as she can remember. Her fascination with words and alphabets began in nursery school where she carried a letter-covered felt book bag. Silly and anachronistic as it sounds, penmanship was one of her favorite grade school subjects. High school and college writing opportunities led to a journalism career. Although she has written about everything from mathematics to mastitis, Vickie's passion is researching and writing about antique needlework. He articles have appeared in many needlework magazines, including *Sampler & Antique Needlework Quarterly* and *Just Cross Stitch*.

She and daughter-in-law Maegan Jennett are partners in NeedleWorkPress, a home-based business dedicated to preserving and presenting printed materials related to historic needlework. In fact, the name NeedleWorkPress incorporates the first initials of her husband's and sons' names: Niles, Willy and Patrick.

Vickie's home and the home of NeedleWorkPress is the replica of a 19th-century farmhouse in the country just outside of metro-Phoenix, AZ, where she and Niles raised two sons, countless calves and a couple of pygmy goats. Now Maegan, Patrick and Zoe live just down the road while Willy, Ashley, Hooper and Van live a quick six-hour drive across the desert in the LA area.

Perhaps Vickie is best characterized by the sentiment stitched on a sampler in her living room: "My faith, my family and my friends bring meaning to my life."

Visit Vickie at her website at
www.needleworkpress.com.